T0078155

He is the Product...
THE ALMIGHTY

Authored By: **Dickens Saint-elien**

WESTBOW
PRESS®
A DIVISION OF THOMAS NELSON
& ZONDERVAN

This book is a work of non-fiction. Unless otherwise noted, the author and the publisher make no explicit guarantees as to the accuracy of the information contained in this book and in some cases, names of people and places have been altered to protect their privacy.

WestBow Press books may be ordered through booksellers or by contacting:

WestBow Press
A Division of Thomas Nelson & Zondervan
1663 Liberty Drive
Bloomington, IN 47403
www.westbowpress.com
1 (866) 928-1240

ISBN: 978-1-5127-7388-0 (sc)
ISBN: 978-1-5127-7387-3 (e)

Library of Congress Control Number: 2017901766

Print information available on the last page.

WestBow Press rev. date: 02/13/2017

Contents

Acknowledgement

First & foremost, I would like to thank _GOD_, my *Heavenly Father &
Creator, a*nd to my *Lord* & Savior _Jesus Christ_, & also to the _Holy Spirit_, for
giving me the *inspiration & motivation* to write this *documentation*. Also I
would like to acknowledge the various *experiences* that I have *encountered*
in my life that gave me the *Knowledge, Wisdom & Understanding* to put
this book together. **"HE IS THE PRODUCT"-THE ALMIGHTY!!!**

*T*HE *A*LMIGHTY "G*O*D"

THE ALMIGHTY INTRODUCTION!!!

When it comes to the *Almighty Creator God*; he does not need an introduction because he is already established. But I will present him to you because he is *Glorious & Worthy* to be *presented*. The *Almighty God* is the *epitome* of *Greatness and Excellence* wrapped in one. He is a *Creator*, a loving *Heavenly Father*, a *Producer*, a *Director*, a Legislator, a Savior, a *Doctor*, a Miracle worker, an *Orchestrator*, a Sustainer, & a *Life giver*. <u>*Just to name a few*</u>.

<u>Matter fact</u>, *He* is the Great *"I Am"* because he can become whatever he chooses to be. He is *Three in One, & 1 in 3*, as the *Holy Trinity*. He is *the <u>Father</u> (Creator), the Son <u>Jesus Christ</u>, (the Redeemer) & the <u>Holy Spirit</u>, (the Comforter)*. He is the *beginning & the end*, the *Alpha & the Omega*. Nobody can live or function outside of him because he is our *Source. OH! Praise Be to God!!!*

The *book* of Genesis in the *Holy Bible mentioned, "In the beginning, God created the Heavens & the Earth". And the earth was without shape & it was empty*. And *God* eventually called life into *existence* & the *creations* on *Earth* became.

God created planet earth for humanity to have a living experience with him, *"Vertically"* and with others, *"Horizontally"*. *The Earth & humanity was created for God's will & for his good pleasure. God* is the giver of *life*; he is the very air that you breathe because he created you. *Life* in its own way is a mystery and the only person that can unravel its hidden *jewels* is the *almighty* himself. *Life* is also a precious gift that should be *appreciated*; as well as fully lived.

Life is a school & we all are here to *develop,* so we can become better individuals.

Life is also a *movie* and we all have a part to play in order to *fulfill our purpose.*

God is the meaning of life, & life without *God has no meaning.* You cannot have one without the other. As a *m*atter of fact, he breathe, the breath of life within humanity & we become *living souls.* Our *body* the *"Soma",* & our *spirit* the *"Pneuma,"* & our *soul* the *"Psuche',* all comes from the *LORD.* *H*umans are a Triune being, which is made up of the *body, spirit & soul.* And the *LORD* is the *Author* of it all.

The *Holy Bible* mentioned that the body will return to the earth where it came from.

And the spirit which represents *life* will come back to *God* who gave it. *God* is the giver of life and nobody can exist outside of him.

This *book "He is the Product"-The Almighty,* was written to give you an insightful understanding of the *prowess* of the *almighty God.* Beside him being your *Creator,* he is also your *providential heavenly father, who blesses, provides, & sustains his Creation.*

God is the primary *s*upplement that you need in order to *function and to live.* Whether you are *a "believer", an "agnostic" or an "atheist"? It does not change* the fact that you need him so you can *survive. God* is the source, which everything originates & comes from. Whether it's your *ethnicity,* the *c*olor of your *skin,* your *personality, your character, your intelligence, your creativity, your abilities, your wisdom, your anointing, or your talent;* it all comes from the *almighty God.*

*H*e is the *Master Creator* who specializes in establishing. None of us chose the *gifts or the talents* that we carry; *God* made that decision without our consent. But he gave it to us for a reason. Now it's up to you & I to *utilize* them. We are *God's* handy worker & it's through us that he accomplishes his plans. *A*ll you got to do is come together with the *almighty*; & then he will do the rest. The *LORD* is your *co-pilot*, who will assist you to your destination of possibility, that's why *"He is the Product"-The Almighty.*

God is not an option, he is a *necessity,* & you need him so you can make it in life. When you accept *God* through his son *Jesus Christ*? Then He will become *your Savior, your Lord, your provider, your supporter, your protector, your healer, your peacemaker, & your way maker.*

Vitamins are supplements that are needed to give your *body* a *boost,* & they also provide *nutrients."Guess what",* God is your *spiritual supplement that will enhance you so you can have a victorious life. T*he *LORD* is the answer to your question, & he is the solution to your problems. Nothing is *too hard, or impossible* for *God* to accomplish. He loves *humanity* because he created the *human race.* <u>He wants the best for them.</u>

<u>So I encourage you</u>, to make *God* a priority in your life. And watch him do mighty things on your behalf. The *Gospel* of *"Matthew 6:33"* say's, *"Seek God's Kingdom first, and his righteousness & everything else will be added to you".*

God is the one who creates for his own pleasure, so he can live out his purpose throughout his creations. Whatever he starts in your life, best believe he will finish it. *R*emember *y*our life is a *gift* from *God* & what you do with it; is your *gift* back to him, **"SO Sit BACK, RELAX & ENJOY!!! "HE IS THE PRODUCT"-THE ALMIGHTY!!!**

GOD

ELOHIM

"THE SUPREME CREATOR"

Selah: 1

THE CREATOR

<u>Definition</u>: *A **<u>Creator</u>** is a person who creates & who initiates something.*

<u>Synonym</u>: *Inventor, Originator, Architect, Author, Father, Initiator, Innovator, Founder, Pioneer, Mastermind;*

<u>(KJV) Genesis 1:1</u>-"In the beginning God created the Heavens & the Earth".

<u>(KJV) Isaiah 40:28</u>-"Hast thou not known? hast thou not heard, that the everlasting God, the LORD, *the Creator of the ends of the earth, fainteth not, neither is weary? there is no searching of his understanding".*

For years now scientist has always questioned the existence of *planet earth* & the *human race*. Some believe in the big bang theory, and others speculated that the human evolution started from the ancestry of apes & monkeys. What scientists failed to realize is the existence of the universe is not merely a natural happenstance, but it's based on a *spiritual* *c*onception.

The human mind can only rational to its finite degree. But when *God* gives you a revelation that comes from his mind; he gives you the ability to comprehend things that others may not understand. Just like when *God* gave *Moses* the *blue print* to write the *book* of the *"Torah"* or the *"Pentateuch"*. Which is the *Hebrew & Greek* word for the first *5 books* of the *Laws* in the *Holy Scriptures?*

Moses received *divine information* from *God* to write these *prolific books*; *especially* the book of *Genesis* which dealt with the origin of *Creation*. What we need to realize is everything in the natural has a beginning & an end. Everything comes from a womb and it is birth out of purpose. The *Almighty God* is the only entity that is *eternal,* because he has no beginning & no end. He was always there & he will continue to be.

God is a spirit who is very intelligent & wise. And he sits on the circle of the earth with all powers in his hands; *as he governs the universe. God* is a thinker who always thought before he act. He is a strategic *God,* who has a master plan for his *Creation*.

The *Almighty God* is the *Creator* of every living *creature & person* on this earth. Nobody can exist outside of him because he is the giver and sustainer of life. If *God* did not will for a person, or a thing to exist then it would not. He is the very air that you breathe and he provides you with vitality so you can function. It is because of his power that you *live, move and have your existence.*

He is the *"ELOHIM"*, the *Supreme Creator* of the *earth,* who called life into being, so *you* can have a human experience. When you think of the word *"Genesis"*, *God* is the meaning of that word because *He* is the *origin* of all. *He* is the *"Omnipotent-Unlimited power"*, the *"Omniscient-All knowing"*, & the *"Omnipresent-Everywhere at the same time"* Creator.

The *book of Genesis* is the *autobiography* of *God's creation*. And it *displays* the way he formulated *planet earth. God* is an *Originator*; which is the reason why, you should never duplicate yourself by trying to be like someone else. He created you to be *original & unique? H*umanity was created in the *image and likeness* of *God,* & we are wonderfully made by him. When it comes to *creating,* the *almighty God* is in a class all by himself. He is the *Most High God,* who sits on high & who watches down low. *He* is the *"Pinnacle"*, the *"Zenith"* & his name is *etched* in the *heavenly places,* & his *trademark* is stamp throughout the *earth.*

The *Almighty created* something out of nothing and made it *very good. He* made the earth for the human race. *"He created them male and female in his image & likeness"*. For his *image* deals with his *attributes*, & his *likeness* allocates the ability for you to function like him, when it comes to being *creative.*

Since we are *created* in *God's image & likeness*; as his creation we are a replica of him. *And it's through him that we shine.*

"EL-ELYON" the *Most High God*, is sovereign & in it's in him that we can put our *trust* in. *He* is our *"True Vine"* through whom we receive our *spiritual nutrients* from.

The *LORD* is a *God* of productivity & he has created you to carry out his legacy throughout the *earth*. He wants *you* to do it by *godly reproduction* by being <u>*fruitful*</u>, <u>*multiplying*</u>, <u>*replenishing*</u>, <u>*subduing*</u> & having <u>*dominion*</u>.

Which was the original mandate that the *LORD* proclaimed for his *creation?* So we can make a difference on the earth by the things that we do. The *Almighty God* is a *manufacturer & a distributor* combined all in one. He *creates* & then sets things in its proper placement.

In the *next chapter* of this book, I am going to elaborate on how *God* put things together as an *orchestrator*. The *LORD creates* & then he strategizes to put it *all together.*

The *Bible* clearly states in the book of *Genesis, that Jehovah* had an intention for his *creation*. Which is the reason why *human beings* are always seeking to know what their purpose is & why they exist?

The *LORD* gave us these desires to want to know why we are here on earth. So we can seek for that information through a *relationship* with him. So why not go to the *product,* who is *God. He* has the *manual to your life.* <u>***"Basic instruction before leaving earth" aka "B.i.b.l.e"***</u>

God breathe <u>*inspiration*</u>, <u>*principles*</u> & <u>*his will*</u> through the *Holy Bible*, so you can have an understanding of what his plan is for your life. He created the *Holy Bible*, which is made up of *"5 books of Laws, 12 History books, 5 books of Poetry & Wisdom, 4 books of Major Prophets & 1 Lamentation, 12* books of Minor Prophets, 4 books of the Gospel, 1 book of Acts, 13 Pauline epistle(letters), 8 books of General letters & 1 book of Revelation".

These <u>66</u> books of *divine inspirations* were put together, so you can have a deeper understanding of *God,* & the plan he has for your *life.* Only a *Creator* can do that. *God* loves his creation so much that he was willing to inspire these; <u>*love*</u> & <u>*relational*</u> letters for your benefit.

The *Almighty God* is the architect of the entire universe. He provides everything that we need in order to *sojourn on planet earth.* He created the <u>*Sun*</u> to give us *energy*; as well as to *brighten up our days.* He created the <u>*Moon*</u> *&* <u>*Stars*</u> to govern our nights, so we can *see & function.* He created the <u>*Air*</u> to provide us oxygen, so we can remain alive. He created <u>*Water*</u> in order to bring balance on earth, as the world revolved on its *axis.*

God knows exactly what we need in order to maintain our existence. For nothing in all *creation* is hidden from *God's* sight. *He* knows us more than we know ourselves; obviously because he created us. When *God formed & created* the *first human beings (Adam & Eve)*, he added everything within & around them to sustain their lives.

God is still at work in the lives of humanity. He gave us a *heart*, two *kidneys*, a *respiratory system* & a *digestive system. He* provided *blood* to flow throughout our *anatomy* to give us *vitality. He* gave us a *head* with a *brain* to function, & to be able to think. S*ight to see, nose to smell, ears to hear & a mouth to eat, and also to talk with.*

He added components to our *bodies*, such as *ligaments, joints, arms, hands, legs, and two feet.* He also gave us the *activities of our limbs*, so we can maneuver around to exercise & to work.

See how *strategic & intelligent God* is. He is *brilliant.* Which is why, *"*<u>*He is the Product-The Almighty*</u>*".* Beside, giving us the vehicle of a body to function on the planet? *He* also deposited *talents, giftings, intelligence, wisdom & understanding* so we can be *creative* as well.

Human beings are *co-creators* because it's through us that *God* creates & gets things done on earth. We were *created* to be *creative* & to *exercise* our *creativeness* in the universe. We come from a *creative God.* ***"Thou art worthy, O Lord, to receive glory and honour and power: for thou hast created all things, and for thy pleasure they are and were created." Revelation 4:11 (KJV)***

ADONAI

"LORD MASTER OF THE UNIVERSE"

Selah: 2

THE DIVINE ORCHESTRATOR

Definition: *An **Orchestrator** is a person who composes or arranges; especially by means of clever or thorough planning or maneuvering:*

(KJV)-Genesis 1:9-"And God said, Let the waters under the heaven be gathered together unto one place, and let the dry land appear: and it was so". (KJV)-Romans 8:28-"And we know that all things work together for good to them that love God, to them who are the called according to his purpose".

The *LORD* is not only powerful but he is an *intelligent God*; full of *wisdom* and *understanding*. He is an *architect* who lays out the blueprint while he sketches out the plan. *Heaven* is his canvas & the *Earth* is his paint brush where he strategized & put things together. It took *God six days* to create the *earth* & within those days he divinely *coordinated* the *Universe* so it can function properly.

The *1st* day *God* made the *Light,* the *2nd* day *God* made the *Firmament* (sky), the *3rd* day *God* made the *Seas,* the *4th* day *God* made the *Sun, Moon & Stars,* the *5th* day *God* made *fish & other Creatures,* & on the *6th* day *God* created *a Human being. And on the 7th day* the *LORD's creation* all came together in *Sequence.*

The *LORD* is a strategist and he knows how to get things done. It's amazing how he pulled the woman out of the rib of a man, and then he knitted them together. From the union of a man & woman, *God* created

a family. The *LORD* is a *mathematician* who is a master in *calculating &
arranging* the right elements that will produce the necessary results.

Look it how he gave *Noah* the instructions & the specifications for building
the *Ark*, so he & his family would be safe from the flood. <u>*The Lord then
said to Noah,*</u> **"Come thou and all thy house into the ark; for thee have I
seen righteous before me in this generation. Of every clean beast thou
shalt take to thee by sevens, the male and his female: and of beasts that
are not clean by two, the male and his female.**

**Of fowls also of the air by sevens, the male and the female; to keep
seed alive upon the face of all the earth. For yet seven days, and I will
cause it to rain upon the earth forty days and forty nights; and every
living substance that I have made will I destroy from off the face of
the earth. And Noah did according unto all that the LORD commanded
him.** <u>**(KJV) Genesis 7:1-5**</u>

God did the same thing when he told *Moses* to build the *Tabernacle* according
to his pattern. Every detail and components that were within the tabernacle
were interrelated with one another. *From the Outer Court, to the Inner
Court, to the Holy Place & to the Holy of Holies* were all *sequentially* in *order*.

To the tools within the *Tabernacle* such as; *the Brazen Altar, the Laver
of Brass, the Golden Lamp stand, the Table of Showbread, the Altar of
Incense, the Veil,* and *the Ark of the Covenant* were divinely orchestrated to
accomplish the <u>*Atonement Act*</u>.

God also became a *seamstress* by designing the garments for the *High Priest*
to wear in the *Tabernacle*. "<u>*Exodus Chapter 25 thru 40*</u>", were all scriptures
based on <u>*instructions & specifications*</u> for building the *Tabernacle*.

The pattern for building the tabernacle was narrowed down to a *tee*. The
LORD also gave *King Solomon* specific instructions to build the *Temple* for
the *Nation of Israel*.

If *the LORD orchestrated* & put things together during *biblical times*; then
certainly he can do it presently in your life. The key of seeing *God* at work

in your life is *trusting* & *obeying* him. Orchestration comes with *trust, obedience* & following the *Lord's lead*. The *Almighty God* does his best work of putting things together when you *"Let go & Let God"*.

When you get so used of always being the one in control, then it can stagnate *God's* orchestration in your life. Sometimes; you got to get out of the way and let the *LORD* work. Remember; before you were born *God* already existed. He was the one who called you into existence for his will. So why not let *God* take the steering wheel and put things together on your behalf. ***Ye have not chosen me, but I have chosen you, and ordained you, that ye should go and bring forth fruit, and that your fruit should remain: that whatsoever ye shall ask of the Father in my name, he may give it you. (KJV) John 15:16***

That's what he does *best, besides creating*, is *orchestrating*. He knows how to connect the *dots* & how to fit the *pieces* to the *puzzle*. He is an expert in *arrangement*.

As an example; he picked out your parents and brought them together. Because he knew combining the two *DNA's* would eventually form the right formula to *create you*.

That's why it is important to be nice to people because *God blesses & orchestrates* through *situations and individuals. Like* the saying goes; *"It's nice to be important, but it's more important to be nice"*. You never know where your blessing may come from, *which* is why it's good to be *kind* to the people you *meet*.

The *LORD* makes things happen in the world through the peoples you encounter. It has always been that way from the beginning of the human existence. *Like I mentioned before;* about *Noah* building the *Ark*, he didn't do it all by himself. *God came up with the blue print for the Ark, & then he orchestrated it through Noah & his family*.

It also *implies* to *Moses and Solomon* in regarding on building the *Tabernacle & Temple*. They had assistance. Orchestration deals with *God's* ability to work through *circumstances & events. And* its manifestations are fulfilled through *peoples & situations.*

The thing that I admired about the *LORD*; he is a *thinker & a strategist.* He thinks before he acts & his acts are based on his *knowledge, wisdom & understanding.* **"Declaring the end from the beginning, and from ancient times the things that are not yet done, saying, My counsel shall stand, and I will do all my pleasure. (KJV) Isaiah 46:10**

He told *Jeremiah* before you were even formed and born I already <u>knew you</u>, <u>ordained</u> you, & <u>sanctified</u> you to be a *Prophet.* Through *Jeremiah's* timeline of being, *God arranged, set* & brought his purpose into *existence. God* knows what he's doing, you got to trust him. Sometimes you may get frustrated & you may feel confuse. But that's when you got to keep the *faith & trust in* the LORD. It's through your frustration moments & storms that *God* usually do his best work in your life. *God* is able to smooth out the rough edges when you least expect it.

I am also speaking from my own experiences. There was a time when I came to a cross road & I didn't understand what was happening in my *life.* I had to *let go & let God* because he knew what he was doing. *Especially* when you are dealing with a shift in your life, let the *LORD* do his thing. And be patient & watch how he works it out for you

I had to learn the shifting & transition that takes place in one's life is usually based on *God's orchestrations.* The *Lord's orchestration* usually brings about *change & elevation. You* may not understand at times whats happening but you got to *keep the faith.*

Faith is *believing God,* when it doesn't make sense. And *trust* is allowing him to be in control when you do not understand what he is up too. *Some* way, somehow *God* knows how to fix the broken pieces. And he knows how to mend them back together, even better than before. So *don't worry,* just trust him; for he is working behind the scenes *o*rchestrating on your behalf.

*T*hroughout the ages *God* has always been the one setting & putting things in motion. *He* is the *Master* in the game of *chess.* And your life & destiny are all in his hand. "So *be anxious for nothing but by prayer and supplication, making your request be known unto him*". All you got to do is acknowledge him & he will direct your path. *Your steps are ordered by him and he already laid out the blueprint to your life.*

The story of *Joseph* in the *bible* was a prime example of that; on how the *LORD* orchestrated the events in his life. *Joseph* was given a revelation by *God* by the age of *Seventeen* that he would be a *ruler*. *Thirteen years later the manifestation of that promise became a reality. Joseph* was *Thirty years old* when he entered the service of *"Pharaoh"-King of Egypt.*

He became 2nd in command to *Pharaoh* in the land of *Egypt*. Every event that took place in his life led to his purpose. *God* was working behind the scenes maneuvering and arranging things to work out for *Joseph's* good.

The *LORD* is able to do the same thing for *you*. All you got to do is trust him & he will bring you into your *promise land. God* knows how to get you where you need to be & on time. He is like a *mailman* that knows *when & where to deliver your package.*

"So never give up", continue to *persevere*. And in due time you will receive *what he has for you*. The *LORD* is a *God* of action & he is very able. He is a *Divine orchestrator* who is great in *arranging & making things happen at the right time. What God has for you, is for you. Rest Assure!!!*

Selah: 3

THE TEACHER

Definition: *A **Teacher** is a person who <u>teaches</u>, <u>instructs</u> & <u>informs</u>.*

<u>(KJV) John 3:2</u>-The same came to Jesus by night, and said unto him, Rabbi, we know that thou art a teacher come from God: for no man can do these miracles that thou doest, except God be with him.

Life is a *school* & the world is our *university*. The instructor of our lives is our heavenly *father God*. *Life* is a journey & we all are here on an expedition to learn from our experiences. Nobody was given a manual on how to live life from the time of their conception. *E*very person on this planet at some point in their lives; either received a *revelation,* or had to figure out what their purpose was. Some people learned it at an early age & others got it later on in their lives.

The human existence is consisted of stages, which leads to a person's *progression*. Without these stages it would be a challenge for you to grow & to progress.

<u>The first stage</u> deals with *<u>birth</u>*, which is *<u>existence</u> & <u>possibility</u>*. *<u>The second stage</u>* deals with *<u>infancy</u> (months-3yrs old)*. *<u>The third stage</u>* deals with *<u>childhood</u> (3yrs-11yrs old)*. *<u>The fourth stage</u>* deals with *<u>adolescence</u> (12yrs -19yrs old)*. *<u>The fifth stage</u>* deals with *<u>young adulthood</u> (20yrs-31yrs old)*. *<u>The sixth stage</u>* deals

with *adulthood (32yrs-60yrs old). And then the last stage* deals with *senior adulthood (65yrs & beyond).*

These different life stages shapes & molds you to be who you are as individuals. The *Almighty God* does not go through stages because he is *eternal.* But he guides you through these stages through *life's lessons.* Every stage a person encounter in their life helps them to grow as individuals.

If you're not growing then there is a problem, because life is about *growth.* When I say *growth,* I'm not just referring to your *physicality?* I'm talking about your *mental and spiritual growth.*

The *LORD* uses your life experiences, such as *trials, tests, challenges, lessons & victories* to help you become better. *Like* the saying goes *"the teacher is always quite in the class room when the student is taking the test".*

The *Almighty God* is a teacher of the *highest rank.* He is the *professor* in the university called *life.* The *LORD* would like for humanity to excel & enhance. Sometimes we may not understand why we go through certain things but *God* knows why. One of the toughest things to do; is to trust *God* in the midst of your circumstances.

The *LORD* is a teacher who instructs well & he knows how to *inform, inspire, motivate, encourage* & *edify.* So you can become a better person. Every stage in the human life was design to assist you so you can grow and be effective. Within those stages deals with *process* which is connected to your *experiences* that shapes your *destiny.*

First you must learn to *crawl* before you can *walk*, then you must learn to *walk* before you can *run.* It's all *steps* and *process*, no *elevator. God* the professor knows how to orchestrate life circumstances to make his creation grow. But it's also up to you, if you want to improve. It is a conscious decision based on your part.

I have learned through my own experiences, it's all about your *perspective* & on how you see things. You can take the good out of a negative situation;

only if you view the *lesson correctly*. I know it's easier said than done, but in the process there is a *lesson* to be *learned*.

Since the beginning of time *God* always teaches through the lives of others, as well as your own. *"For a wise person learns from his or her mistakes; & a wiser person learns from others"*.

None of us has gotten to the point where we have mastered the art of *life living*. A person might be more mature than another in their decision making. But we are still *striving & learning* as individuals. Like the *Apostle Paul* said, **"Not as though I had already attained, either were already perfect: but I follow after, if that I may apprehend that for which also I am apprehended of Christ Jesus. (KJV) Philippians 3:12**, *& then he goes to say that "the race is not for the swift, but it's for those who endure it" through perseverance.*

Life is a race but you have to run it with *endurance*. You can't rush it & you cannot be slow either. You got to do it with diligence and with a pace. *God's* methods of teachings are taught with a steady pace. He knows your *strengths* & your *weaknesses*. And he knows what to do in order to help you to *improve*.

For God's Grace is sufficient for you & his strength is made perfect in your weaknesses. That's a comforting statement, just knowing that you can rely on the *LORD*'s grace to help you to make it through. Some things, *God* will bring you out of, & other things he will bring you through it. *Just so you can grow and learn from it.*

Every stage of your life will *assist* you to get to the *next level*. The next level deals with elevation. For every platform of growth prepares & enables you to succeed. You didn't come out of your Mother's womb & then go straight into accomplishing. You had to go through the steps in order for you to get there.

As an example: *You were nursed as an infant, & then comes Day care, then Kindergarten, & then Elementary, then Junior high school, then High school & then College & possibly Graduate school.*

The LORD takes you through process of learning to help your mind develop. From the highest level of schooling in life which is called a *University?* Where you get the root word <u>*universe*</u>, aka <u>*planet earth*</u> or the <u>*world?*</u> *God* uses the universe to teach you lessons so you can grow. As individuals being shaped & molded into *becoming.*

The *almighty God* teaches you life lessons to help you to become *mature.* Just like *Jesus Christ,* the *Rabbi* taught his disciples "<u>The *Sermon on the Mountain*</u>". *Which is based on life principles and lessons?* These kingdom principle teachings that *Jesus* taught benefitted the disciples later on in their lives. "<u>*And guess what*</u>", these teachings are still *relevant & applicable* for you till this day. That's how much *God* loves & cares about you. He wants you to be equipped for life living so you can excel and make it. <u>*Check out*</u>-"*Sermon on the Mount*"-<u>*The Gospel of Matthew Chapters 5 & 6 & 7*</u> in the *Holy Bible.*

In the class called life the student cannot make it without the *instruction* of his *teacher.* The teacher knows what's best for his students. It is the fathers good pleasure to see his children advance in life; <u>*spiritually*</u> *&* <u>*naturally.*</u> The *LORD* does not give you a test to fail you, but he gives it to you so you can progress. He wants you to do well; especially in the area of your <u>*character.*</u> The *Lord* wants you to have honors in <u>*integrity,*</u> as well as in <u>*dignity.*</u> **"I will instruct thee and teach thee in the way which thou shalt go: I will guide thee with mine eye." <u>(KJV) Psalm 32:8</u>**

The school of life is real and there is no exemption from it. Usually the experiences you go through helps you to become stronger. When *Jesus* was "*12 years* old" he was studying with the scholars in the temple. And when he became "*30 years* of age" he began to spearhead his *ministry.*

See the difference from *twelve to thirty years old.* *Jesus* grew in the process that prepared him for his ministry. The *eighteen years* gap, from *12 years of age to 30,* was preparing him for his purpose; *which revolutionized the world.*

God used process to develop *Jesus Christ* for his destiny. *Till* this day, *Jesus Christ* legacy lives on because of his effectiveness when he was on the earth.

The *Lord* gave us *hope & a blessed assurance* that we can receive salvation from him in order to make it into *heaven*. The *Lord* also left us with a *biblical manuscript* called the *"Holy Bible"*. So we can always *read & learn from*, so we can grow *spiritually, as well as naturally*. What a great teacher we have? *The Almighty aka The LORD!!!*

JEHOVAH-JIREH

Selah: 4

THE PROVIDER

Definition: A **Provider** is a person that takes cares of the necessity of others.

(KJV) Genesis 22:8-"And Abraham said, My son, God will provide himself a lamb for a burnt offering: so they went both of them together."

God has a responsibility just like any other parent when it comes to their children. Beside *God* being the *Creator* who created the earth, he is also a providing heavenly father who takes cares of his *creation*. Whatever the LORD creates he will make a way to provide for. *God* is not an irresponsible father who creates without providing.

"And why take ye thought for raiment? Consider the lilies of the field, how they grow; they toil not, neither do they spin: And yet I say unto you, That even Solomon in all his glory was not arrayed like one of these. Wherefore, if God so clothe the grass of the field, which today is, and tomorrow is cast into the oven, shall he not much more clothe you" (KJV) Matthew 6:28-30

Nothing takes *God* by surprise because he already knows what you need before you even ask. But he still appreciates it when you take the time to seek & to ask him. God wants to bless you with your needs, as well as the things that you want. Because he understands that you have desires. But of course even the things that you want; he also wants them to be good for you. *"Delight thyself also in the LORD: and he shall give thee the desires of thine heart". (KJV) Psalm 37:4*

My point is, *God* establishes provisions for each & every one of his children before hand. And these provisions come through many different channels of *resources; whether* it be from *"your giftings", or from "your abilities"* that he has placed within you.

He can also provide for you *suddenly* by performing a *miracle;* just like he did when he *fed* the *5 thousand hungry souls-"by multiplying the 2 fishes & the 5 loaves of bread".* Just so your needs can be met. For your *heavenly father* is *very able & accessible* to provide for your necessities.

God specializes in the *art of provision* because it is his trademark. *And* he does it *well. He* is *"Jehovah-Jireh"* aka the LORD that *Provides.* Just like how he did for *Abraham,* by *providing* the *ram in the bush* to be sacrificed instead of his son *Isaac.*

The *LORD* is always on time & precise when it comes to his provisions. He also did the same by providing for the world when he gave his only *begotten Son, "Jesus Christ"* to die *for the sins of humanity. What* am I suggesting, is whatever you are in need of *God* is capable of making it happen. Throughout the bible he always provided for those who were in need. What a heavenly father that we have who is sensitive enough to know & to feel the burdens of your *necessities.*

For it is the father's good pleasure to give you the *kingdom, and its inheritance.*

As *God's* children he is able to supply your every need. *God* loves his creation and he wants the best for them, *just like any parent would.*

The *providence of God* is extensive because he *governs the entire universe,* and he takes cares of his *belongings.* His *providential care* can also be seen throughout the events that took place in the *Holy Bible. He* is the *source* of all, from *the trees, to the grass, to the birds of the air & also to the human kind.*

The affirmation of *God's providence* identifies his loving care for the dependency of all creation on planet earth. It denies the idea that the universe is governed by chance or happenstance. The *almighty God* is the one who is in control & he is the absolute *provider for all.*

The book of *Genesis* gives you a glimpse of how *God* created & established the earth for the comfort of *humanity*. It took *God* six days to create the earth with all of its natural *resources and supplements*. The *LORD* is intelligent and he knows what we are in need of because he created us. He already determined the things to provide us with so we can live on *earth*. The LORD is a sufficient provider who prepares beforehand so needs can be *met*.

Here are the necessities that are essential for the human existence so they can survive on the earth. *Money, food, clothes & shelter* for *life living*. We all have the potential to acquire these essentials through our *aptitude & talents* that the LORD has supplied us with. *God* has already planted in us *seeds of giftings* so we can *survive & make it on planet earth.*

He also gave us *knowledge, wisdom, understanding, intelligence, health, strength, imagination & a mind to be creative.* Now it's up to you to utilize them so you can make your life work. *God* has *provided* you with these tools to help you be productive so you can reap a *bountiful harvest.*

Just like how *God* provided for the *birds of the air* with *twigs* so they can build their nest. He gave them the materials, now it's up to them to go find them & utilize it. *It's* like teaching a person how to fish; so they can continue to feed themselves. *God* has many different ways to provide for you. He can do it *naturally or supernaturally.*

As an example; If you need *money* to buy food & to pay your bills? The *LORD* will give you *a job*, or an *opportunity*, or *a talent*, or even your *own business*. So your needs can be *fulfilled*.

And if you need a mate to share your life with then *God* will introduce you to your *spouse*. The *Lord* will supply your need in every area of your *life.* All you got to do is, *"Ask & it will be given to you, Seek & you will find, Knock & the doors will be open".*

Remember, nothing is too hard or impossible for *God* to do. He is the *"EL-SHADDAI"* the *All Sufficient One.* He can provide you with *healing,* if you are sick. "He can provide you with *protection* if you need safety". "He can provide you with *strength* if you are weak". "He can provide you with *peace* in the midst of your storm." "He can provide you with *favor* so doors of opportunity can open for you". *Must I continue: I hope you get my point!!!*

Whatever you need he can provide it. The *LORD* is a *God* of <u>*addition &*</u> <u>*multiplication*</u>. *Subtraction and division* are not in his vocabulary when it comes to providing for his *creation. God* wants your soul to prosper in every aspect of your life. So never settle for less when you can have *God's best.* The *LORD* wants you to have more than enough. *Not lacking anything-* **Behold, He struck the rock, So that the waters gushed out, and the streams overflowed.** <u>**(KJV) Psalm 78:20**</u>

He is the *God* of *abundance* & sufficiency who will go beyond the measure to provide for you. Just like how he provided manna from heaven & the water from the rock to meet the needs of his people *"Israel". He will also do it for you.*

"He is the bread of life, whoever comes to him will never hunger; and whoever believes in him will never thirst". He is not only the *God of Abraham, Isaac & Jacob,* but he is also your *God,* who will sustain you. For he cares for you just like a parent to its children. *He* sits on high & who watches down low to make sure that the earth is being *supervised.* **"Thou visitest the earth, and waterest it: thou greatly enrichest it with the river of God, which is full of water: thou preparest them corn, when thou hast so provided for it. Thou waterest the ridges thereof abundantly: thou settlest the furrows thereof: thou makest it soft with showers: thou blessest the springing thereof. Thou crownest the year with thy goodness; and thy paths drop fatness".** <u>**(KJV) Psalm 65:9-11**</u>

See, what I mean he takes care of the earth and his creation. He does not only just create & leaves it up to you to figure it out. But he plays his position as a responsible *Heavenly Father*. He is the prince of life who sustains life through *provision*.

God is a visionary who sees the end from the beginning because He is *eternal*.

He knows *the beginning, the middle & the end* of every human existence. The *LORD* already predetermined provision for humanity before the foundation of the world.

God knows all because he is *omniscient*. <u>*Truth be told*</u>; he knows the amount of hairs that's on your head, & they all are numbered. That's how much he is in touch with your existence. *God* is concerned with every area of your being. Which is why, you should always seek, & have him to be the priority of your *life*.

As a child of God, it is imperative that you maintain your relationship with him.

Not because he is able to provide for you, but because he is your very existence.

You need him in order to exist & live. Your *physical body* that houses your *spirit* & *soul*, was provided from *God*, so you can operate on earth. Within your body he gave you 5 senses to *experience life*; through *touching, smelling, tasting, hearing & seeing*.

Beside him providing for you in the *natural*; he also gives you things that pertain for your *spiritual enrichment*. Such as the "*Fruit of the Holy Spirit*", which are *Love, Joy, Peace, Faithfulness, Goodness, Kindness, Gentleness, Self-control & Patience?* *God* wants you to be *spiritually* & *naturally fit*. The *Almighty God* is like a *multi-vitamin* that caters to your *whole being*. So you can function *well*.

The *children* of *Israel* witness *God's* provision when they were in the wilderness. The *LORD* provided for them by a *pillar of cloud*, & by a *pillar of fire* to guide them. He also made provision for them through the *working of miracles* to bring them out of *Egypt*, & into their *Promise Land*.

God supply's never runs out because is he is the source of life. He *creates, produces & supplies* the *demands*. Whether it be; *strength, guidance or protection?* **"O taste and see that the LORD is good: blessed is the man that trusteth in him". (KJV) Psalm 34:8**

➢ *Here are 10 spiritual provisions from the LORD*

➢ The *1ˢᵗ* **provision** is the gift of ***Salvation***
   that comes from *Jesus Christ*.

"Neither is there salvation in any other: for there is none other name under heaven given among men, whereby we must be saved". (KJV) Acts 4:12

"For I know that this shall turn to my salvation through your prayer, and the supply of the Spirit of Jesus Christ," (KJV) Philippians 1:19

"For God did not appoint us to wrath, but to obtain salvation through our Lord Jesus Christ"-(KJV) 1 Thessalonians 5:9

➢ The *2ⁿᵈ* provision is ***Eternal Life***.

"For God so loved the world, that he gave his only begotten Son, that whosoever believeth in him should not perish, but have everlasting life."-(KJV) John 3:16

"And I give unto them eternal life; and they shall never perish, neither shall any man pluck them out of my hand." -(KJV) John 10:28

"And this is life eternal, that they might know thee the only true God, and Jesus Christ, whom thou hast sent."- (KJV) John 17:3

➢ The ***3ʳᵈ* provision** is the gift of the ***Holy Spirit***.

"And, being assembled together with them, commanded them that they should not depart from Jerusalem, but wait for the promise of the Father, which, saith he, ye have heard of me." -(KJV) Acts 1:4

"And they were all filled with the Holy Ghost, and began to speak with other tongues, as the Spirit gave them utterance."-(KJV) Acts 2:4

"In whom ye also trusted, after that ye heard the word of truth, the gospel of your salvation: in whom also after that ye believed, ye were sealed with that holy Spirit of promise,"-(KJV) Ephesians 1:13

➢ The ***4ᵗʰ* provision** is his ***Mercy***.

"But the LORD was with Joseph, and shewed him mercy, and gave him favour in the sight of the keeper of the prison". -(KJV) Genesis 39:21

"Thou in thy mercy hast led forth the people which thou hast redeemed: thou hast guided them in thy strength unto thy holy habitation". -(KJV) Exodus 15:13

"And when he heard that it was Jesus of Nazareth, he began to cry out, and say, Jesus, thou son of David, have mercy on me."- (KJV) Mark 10:47

➢ The ***5ᵗʰ* provision** is his ***Grace***.

"And the LORD said unto Moses, I will do this thing also that thou hast spoken: for thou hast found grace in my sight, and I know thee by name".-(KJV) Exodus 33:17

"And the child grew, and waxed strong in spirit, filled with wisdom: and the grace of God was upon him".-(KJV) Luke 2:40

"For the law was given by Moses, but grace and truth came by Jesus Christ".-(KJV) John 1:7

➢ The *6ᵗʰ* **provision** is the gift of ***Faith***.

"To another faith by the same Spirit; to another the gifts of healing by the same Spirit;"-(KJV) 1 Corinthians 12:9

"We having the same spirit of faith, according as it is written, I believed, and therefore have I spoken; we also believe, and therefore speak;"-(KJV) 2 Corinthians 4:13

➢ The *7ᵗʰ* **provision** is ***Preservation***.

"And God sent me before you to preserve you a posterity in the earth, and to save your lives by a great deliverance".-(KJV) Genesis 45:7

"Thou shalt keep them, O LORD, thou shalt preserve them from this generation forever".-(KJV) Psalm 12:7

"And the Lord shall deliver me from every evil work, and will preserve me unto his heavenly kingdom: to whom be glory for ever and ever. Amen".-(KJV) 2 Timothy 4:18

➢ The *8ᵗʰ* **provision** is ***Healing***.

"And the people, when they knew it, followed him: and he received them, and spake unto them of the kingdom of God, and healed them that had need of healing".-(KJV) Luke 9:11

"To another faith by the same Spirit; to another the gifts of healing by the same Spirit;"-(KJV) 1 Corinthians 12:9

➢ The *9ᵗʰ* **provision** to you is ***Anointing***.

"This is the portion of the anointing of Aaron, and of the anointing of his sons, out of the offerings of the LORD made by fire, in the day when he presented them to minister unto the LORD in the priest's office;"-(KJV) Leviticus 7:35

"But the anointing which ye have received of him abideth in you, and ye need not that any man teach you: but as the same anointing teacheth you of all things, and is truth, and is no lie, and even as it hath taught you, ye shall abide in him".-(KJV) 1 John 2:27

➢ The **_10ᵗʰ_ provision** to you is **_Wisdom_**.

"And I have filled him with the spirit of God, in wisdom, and in understanding, and in knowledge, and in all manner of workmanship,"-(KJV) Exodus 31:3

"For to one is given by the Spirit the word of wisdom; to another the word of knowledge by the same Spirit;"-(KJV) 1 Corinthians 12:8

The *LORD* is a *God* of provision and his barrel is always full with plenty. **_"Even by the God of thy father, who shall help thee; and by the Almighty, who shall bless thee with blessings of heaven above, blessings of the deep that lieth under, blessings of the breasts, and of the womb:" (KJV) Genesis 49:25_**

Selah: 5

THE WAY MAKER

*Definition: A **Way maker** creates an opportunity despite of opposition and difficulties. In other words they will make a way out of no way, no matter the situation.*

(KJV) Exodus 13:18-But God led the people about, through the way of the wilderness of the Red sea: and the children of Israel went up harnessed out of the land of Egypt. (KJV) 1 Corinthians 10:13-There hath no temptation taken you but such as is common to man: but God is faithful, who will not suffer you to be tempted above that ye are able; but will with the temptation also make a way to escape, that ye may be able to bear it.

Throughout history it has been proven that our *Creator* has always been instrumental for making ways for his people. He is the ladder that will help you get to the top, & he is the bridge that will get you over to the other side. Let's take a trip back to memory lane in the book of *Exodus* in the bible, during the time when *Israel* as a Nation, was held in captivity in *Egypt*.

To make a long story short-The *LORD* through his servant *Moses* performed miracles & brought *Israel* out of slavery from *Egypt*. *God* did whatever it took for him to set his people *free*. From sending ten plagues to Pharaoh's house & to opening upon the *Red Sea*, so *Israel* can come out. **"And Moses said unto the people, Remember this day, in which ye came out from Egypt, out of the house of bondage; for by strength of hand**

the LORD *brought you out from this place: there shall no leavened bread be eaten." (KJV) Exodus 13:3*

The LORD was concerned about the liberty of Israel and he did whatever it took to make that happen. If *God* did it for *Israel*, then he can also do it for you. When it seems like your back is up against the wall & there is no hope; that's when *God* will step in your situation. *Matter of fact*; he will open up the Red sea in your problems, so he can bring you out.

Life at times can get quite challenging but you got to keep the faith. And believe that the *LORD* will make a way. *God* is strategic and he knows how to deliver you. Just like how he did for *Apostle Peter* by bringing him out from prison. The *LORD* will go to the extent to make ways so he can set you free, but you got to do your part. When the *Apostle Peter* was locked in prison the bible said that *"the church prayed earnestly"* & then *God* went to work on his *behalf.* So it's a *two-fold act*; *the (church prayed), and then (God made it happen).*

So whatever you're going through, *pray fervently* so the *LORD* can move on your *behalf. Prayer* is the *key* that will propel the *LORD* to solve your problems. Whatever you are dealing with that is unpleasant, pray to *God* about it? Communicating with the *LORD* is the stepping stone to your *deliverance. As* you pray, you must also believe that *God* can & that he will. The *acronym* for *(P.U.S.H)-"Pray Until Something Happens" or "Praise Until Something Happens"*

God rewards those who seeks him earnestly; in other words when you pursue *God* with a steadfast mental attitude of believing; then he will start walking on the water to your circumstances. The *LORD* is concerned about your deliverance & he wants you to be free. One of the ways the *LORD* gets glory in your *life* is when you are *prevailing & progressing.* When the *LORD's* hand is on your life, none of your enemies can stand before you & stop you.

God will fight your battles and bring you out on *Eagles* wings. He will make your foes become your *foot stool.* And he will also prepare a table in the presence of your enemies, so they can watch you *succeed. God* will create opportunities and open doors that nobody can shut. *OH! Glory be to GOD!!! That's how Mighty & Great God is.*

The Lord also brought the *Apostle Paul and Silas* out from prison because of their trust in him. They *prayed & sung hymns* unto the *Lord* & he made a way out for them. The *Almighty God* is a way maker who will tear the hinges off the doors & cut the roof top open, *just so you can get out.*

*N*ever underestimate what God can do to bring you out on the other side. *Despite* what you are going through in your life, always keep a *hopeful view. Trust me*; I know because I am speaking based on my own experiences. On how the *LORD* brought me out of homelessness and difficulties. He gave me the *victory* over my circumstances & my enemies.

*H*e will make a way for you too; whether it's *financially,* or just opening doors of *opportunities,* so you can *achieve* & *move forward. Especially*; when it comes to your *soul? Look it* how he made a way for humanity to receive salvation so they can be *saved* through *Jesus Christ.* Over 2000 years ago *God* sent *Jesus Christ* on the earth to die for the sins of humanity.

*B*eside the *LORD* making a way so you can prosper in your endeavors, he has also made a way for you to be *saved* from your sins. The *LORD* wants you to inherit *eternal life,* which starts now on *earth* & it continues in *heaven. God* wants you to be *saved,* so you can have a relationship with him. *God* is a loving heavenly father who cares about his creation and he wants the best for them; especially their *freedom.*

"Jesus Christ", *God's* only begotten son was the only person who was qualified to become the *atoning* sacrifice for sin. And he provided a way to save fallen humanity. He came to earth and was born as a baby. His earthly *Mother* was *Mary,* & his *heavenly Father* is the *almighty God. Jesus*; therefore did not have the sinful nature of man, but the sinless nature of *God.*

Jesus lived *thirty three & a half years* on earth, and did not sin once. *He* was the *"Lamb of God"* who took away the sins of the world. *God* made a way to save human beings through *Christ* because he loves us. *God* is the only *source* of product that creates *something out of nothing.* He is an *innovative creator.* He will open up the *Red Sea & the Jordan River* at the same time to bring you to your *promise land.* That's what a way maker does, is provide the opportunity so you can be bless. **"It is God that girdeth me with strength, and maketh my way perfect." (KJV) Psalm 18:32**

Look at what he did for *Joseph,* how he brought him out from the pit to the *palace.* <u>Like</u> I stated <u>previously</u>, when your back is up against the wall, then the *LORD* will make a way for you. *All you got to do is* "<u>Stand still & see his Salvation</u>"

> ➤ ***Here is a list of some of the people-The Almighty God made a way for.***

He made a way for <u>*Noah & his family*</u> to be *saved* from the flood-<u>*2 Peter 2:5*</u>

He made a way for <u>*Moses & the Nation of Israel*</u> from slavery-<u>*Exodus 14:13-16*</u>

He made a way for <u>*Joseph & for the 12 Tribe of Israel*</u> to survive the famine-<u>*Gen 45:3-8*</u>

He made a way for <u>*King David*</u> to gain the victory over Goliath-<u>*1Samuel 17:45-47*</u>

He made a way for the <u>*3 Hebrew boys*</u> *(Shadrach, Meshach & Abednego)*-<u>*Daniel 3:16-30*</u>

He made a way for <u>*King Hezekiah*</u> to overcome the king of Assyria-<u>*2 Kings 19:5-7*</u>

He made a way for <u>*Nehemiah*</u> to rebuild the walls of Jerusalem-<u>*Nehemiah 4:7-9*</u>

He made a way & delivered <u>*Daniel*</u> from the Lion's den-<u>*Daniel 6:18-23*</u>

He made a way for <u>*Apostle Peter & Apostle Paul & Silas*</u> out of prison-<u>*Acts 12:5-11 & Acts 16:25-28*</u>

He made the ultimate way for *Humanity* through his *Son Jesus Christ* who died for the remissions of human beings-*John 3:16-17 & Romans 5:8*

The *Almighty Creator* will always make a way for his children; especially when it comes to their purpose based on his will for their lives. *God (ABBA)* is a true deliverer who will back up his *promises* & *he can do it all by himself.*

All you got to do is believe and watch him do it. Always keep the faith, and *never give in, never breakdown & never give up*. "*For your redemption draws nigh because he is your light & your salvation. God* did it back then during the *biblical times* & he is still making ways for his children up till this day. *What a mighty God we serve!!!*

YAHWEH
"THE SELF-EXISTENT GOD"

Selah: 6

THE MIRACLE WORKER

Definition: **Miracle** *is a supernatural act of God; it is the LORD, God acting on your behalf.*

(KJV) Deuteronomy 11:3-And his miracles, and his acts, which he did in the midst of Egypt unto Pharaoh the king of Egypt, and unto all his land;"

(KJV) Acts 2:22-Ye men of Israel, hear these words; Jesus of Nazareth, a man approved of God among you by miracles and wonders and signs, which God did by him in the midst of you, as ye yourselves also know:

In biblical times the *almighty God* always dealt with two establishments of miracles. One of them is based on the *"Gift of faith".* And the other is through the *"Working of miracles".*

Both of these miraculous acts were part of the *spiritual gifts* that the *LORD* has bestowed upon the church. The *Greek* meaning for miracle in the *New Testament* is the word *"semeion"* (*pronounced*) *say-mi-on.*, *which* means *"sign or wonder".*

The *spiritual gifts* of *"working of miracles" & "the gift of faith"* can be located in *1 Corinthians 12:4-1.* This passage of scripture deals with the *diversities of gifts* that the *Lord* distributed to his *Church* (*the body of Christ*).

The Greek term for spiritual gifts is *"pneumatikos"*, which is *synonymous* to the word *"charisma"*, which means *"gift"*. *And* it is also akin to the word *"charis"*, which means *grace*. For these spiritual *gift's* were gracefully given to the body of *Christ* to strengthen the *church* & to help it *progress*.

Let's begin with the *"gift of faith"*, which is one of the highest spiritual gifts that you can obtain. The *"gift of faith"* is powerful because it causes the *LORD* to act on your behalf, & it is based on your *belief*.

The *second* spiritual gift is the *"working of miracles"* which allows the *LORD* to work through you to perform miracles. I just wanted to give you some background on how the *LORD* deals with miracles through these spiritual gifts. But my point is not based on these *giftings* but rather the miracle itself.

<u>*As an example*</u>-When the *LORD* used *Moses* to stretch out his rod to open up the *Red Sea* for the deliverance of the Nation of *Israel*. These acts that took place through *Moses* were known as the *working of miracles*.

<u>But on the other hand</u>, when *Jesus Christ* raised *Lazarus* from the dead, & when he turned water into wine, those miracles were based on the *gift of faith*.

These two examples of miracles were done on two different bases, but was still acted upon *God's supernatural doing*. The point that I am suggesting is regardless of which base it's acted upon; the miracle still comes from the *almighty God. For he is the one that causes the miracle to happen!!!*

Throughout the dispensation ages; whether *biblically or historically*, God has always been there performing miracles. The *LORD* is always working, and he is still in the business of the miraculous. Some people may believe, & others may not, but *"guess what"* I can testify that *God* still performs miracles.

Miracles shouldn't be categorized, whether *small or big* because it is based on the need. But nevertheless, it's still a miracle. Just like when *Jesus* multiplied the *2 fishes & the 5 loaves of bread*, or better yet when he healed the *leper.* The act of these miracles weren't the same but the needs of them were met.

The *Almighty* can do *exceedingly & abundantly* beyond all that you can even imagine. The *LORD* is an expert when it comes to the miraculous. He is a miracle worker; who can perform miracles based on your situation? It all depends on your faith. If you have *faith,* as small as a mustard seed, then the *LORD* will do great things for you. ***"And the Lord said, If ye had faith as a grain of mustard seed, ye might say unto this sycamine tree, Be thou plucked up by the root, and be thou planted in the sea; and it should obey you." (KJV) Luke 17:6***

The *LORD* does not run out of miracles because he *manufactures* them. He will put the *super* in your *natural* & then comes the *miracle.* It is also imperative that you understand that miracles usually happen in *God's* timing. Having faith in *God* also requires faith in his timing. Some miracles he can make happen *"suddenly",* right on the spot, & others happens on *"God's timetable".*

So if you are expecting a miracle from the *LORD,* & you haven't receive what you prayed for; *just wait & give it some time.* Do not lose hope; it's on its way. Some miracles take time because it is based of *God's* orchestration. But have no worries, he will deliver. For the *acronym* for **"_G.O.D_" is "_Guaranteed "On time" Deliverer_".** When *Jesus* performed miracles while he was on earth they were précised; as well as on time.

Throughout the *Holy Scriptures God* always made a statement with the miraculous. Whether it was *defending his children, or providing for them.* He always made an impact that resonated through the *supernatural.* Miracles are also derived by *power;* which is known as the *"dunamis".*

"Dunamis" is a *Greek* word and it means, *"act of power"* or *"miraculous power"* or the *"ability to do".* It is an inherent power which produces results. The *LORD* is a *God* of action and he has the power to make it happen. *Remember* the *LORD* is an extraordinary *GOD,* who acts beyond the laws of nature. No event in the course of *God's providence* can be traced to the

agency of man. Because it is *God* acting upon nature to accomplish what he is able to do.

➤ *Miracles produces breakthroughs* & breakthrough opens doors.

Our Lord Jesus Christ also appealed to miracles as a conclusive proof of his divine mission. Therefore the person that the *LORD* works miracles through, clearly states that they have the authority of *God*. And they have the credentials to back it up as being *the LORD's agent*.

This is the reason why *God* is the product of it all, because he is the one that initiates the miracle to take place. Without him you have no miracle. He has the final say on how to perform it, & also when to display it. The *LORD* is the architect of it all and he has the capability to manifest it.

Just like how he brought *Israel* out of Egypt with his *almighty hand*. Whatever it takes to accomplish his purpose, the *LORD* will do it. In the *New Testament* miracles were performed to make non-believers believe. In *biblical times*; *Christ* won many souls through the act of miracles. The miracles *Jesus* performed were for his *public ministry*. Because he understood the *scriptural principle*; **"The fruit of the righteous is a tree of life; and he that winneth souls is wise."-(KJV) Proverbs 11:30**

Miracles usually carry out *God's* purpose. It is *God's* intervention in the life of human kind. Miracles are also known as *signs and wonders*. **"And by the hands of the apostles were many signs and wonders wrought among the people;-(KJV) Acts 5:12**

One of the valuable way's to understand miracles is to examine the various terms for miracles in the bible. *Like I mentioned before, signs and wonders* were *biblical terms* that demonstrated the acts of the miraculous. *Jesus Christ*, as well as his apostles had many signs & wonders followed them because they were *"approved by God"*.

The LORD chosen servants, especially in the *Old Testament* had many *signs and wonders* followed them. *God* is still able to address miracles even till this day. *Just* being *alive* is a miracle all by itself. Being able to *breathe and to have the activities of your limbs*; as well as the functioning of your *organs* is a miracle.

The human heart beats, <u>100,000 times</u> *per day,* and about <u>35 million times *in a year*</u>. During an average lifetime, the human heart will beat more than <u>2.5 billion times</u>. So see what I mean, you're not even aware how many times your heart beats per day. But the *LORD* is the one who manages your heart rate, as he keeps you *alive & well.*

Give a tennis ball a good hard squeeze. You're using about the same amount of force your heart uses to pump blood out to your body. Now tell me if that's not a miraculous act of *God*. <u>*OH! Glory Be to GOD!!!*</u>

> *The Almighty God performed <u>35 miracles</u> through Jesus Christ in the <u>New Testament</u>-But they were more miracles from the Lord that weren't mentioned.*

> *<u>Total of Miracles performed in the entire Holy Bible by</u> The Almighty God were more than <u>100 miracles</u>*

Selah: 7

THE BLESSER

Definition: *God is a **Blesser** who bestows good and who invokes favor upon.*

(KJV) Genesis 12:2-And I will make of thee a great nation, and I will bless thee, and make thy name great; and thou shalt be a blessing:

(KJV) Psalm 29:11-The LORD will give strength unto his people; the LORD will bless his people with peace.

When the *LORD* wanted to create a nation he chose one man to do it. *Biblically* speaking, the man he chose was *Abram,* who later became *Abraham. God* has pronounced "*7 Promises of blessings*" unto *Abraham.*

Here is a list of the "Seven Promises" that the LORD has declared unto his servant Abraham, & to those who are Abraham seed through Jesus Christ. Genesis Chapter 12, verse 1-3,

1. *I will show you a land. (which will be yours & your descendants)*

2. *I will make you into a Great Nation.*

3. *I will Bless You.*

4. *I will make your Name Great.*

5. *I will cause you to be a Blessing.*

6. *I will Bless them that bless you & I will curse them that curse you.*

7. *In you all of the family of the earth will be Bless.*

- God made *Abraham* these promises because he wanted to bless him and his descendants. The *LORD's* promises are always attach with a blessing.

- *As a matter of fact* he said that, *"He is not slacked in concerning the promises that he makes"*. The same promises that *God* made to *Abraham* also pertains to a *born again* believer. Because you are *Abrahams* seed through *Jesus Christ.*

The *blessing* of the *LORD* stems from *Generation to generations*. The *LORD* is a *God* of *Generation* because he works through peoples. *Abraham* was not the only person throughout the scriptures in the bible that *God* made a covenant of blessings with. He also promised to bless *Noah & his family*; as well as *Isaac, Jacob, King David, King Solomon & countless of others in the Holy bible.*

The *LORD* enjoys blessing his children. He takes pleasure in doing so. If you are a *child of God*, then being bless makes him *look good. God* is glorified when *you & I* are *blessed. "As children of the Most High God, we are heirs with him & joint heirs with our Lord Christ"*. And because of that, we are entitled to receive the blessings that he has promised *Abraham*. Which are *spiritual & natural blessings-*

God's blessings are *spiritual*; as well as *natural.* The *blessings* that we receive; as *born again* believers can be found in *Ephesians 1:4-13.*

The word *blessing* in the book of *Ephesians 1:3* is the *Greek word "eulogeo"*, and it means *"to speak well of" & "to celebrate with praises"*, the *LORD* is the one acting in this verse, *pronouncing good things unto us.*

> ➢ *Here is a list of blessings that God has decreed towards his church (the body of Christ)-Ephesians Chapter 1 & 2*

The *1ˢᵗ* blessing deals with the *election as Saints*, in *Ephesians 1:4*, says that He has "chosen us in him before the foundation of the world, that we should be holy and without blame before him in love. *"God has chosen to make us holy and blameless, and all because of his love, his good pleasure, and his grace"*

What a blessing, that "even when we were dead in our sins" *God* chose to extend his grace to us and offer us salvation. This is even more amazing when you realize that He made that decision to bless us despite our shortcomings. *Ephesians 2:5,*

The *2ⁿᵈ* blessing listed is found in *verse 5; Our adoption as his children.* Not only has *God* chosen us to be made *holy*, but He grants us full status as His children, with all the benefits thereof. *(KJV) John 1:12* says, **"But as many as received him, to them gave he power to become the sons of God, even to them that believe on his name:"** *When we believe the gospel, we receive full access to the Father, being able to call out to him as his children.*

The *3ʳᵈ* blessing in *verse 6*, where we are made to be *"accepted in the beloved."* He makes us graceful or favorable through *Christ*, as the *beloved of God*. Because of *Christ*, the Father sees his loveliness when He looks at us. The *blood of Christ* has taken away the guilt of our sins, and we stand before the Father as perfectly accepted.

This leads us right into the *4ᵗʰ* blessing (*Ephesians 1:7*), *the redemption through his blood*. Redemption speaks of buying one's freedom, paying a ransom. The price for our sins, the payment to buy us out of eternal condemnation, was fully paid by the *blood of Christ.*

In *Christ,* we are no longer slaves to sin, but we become slaves to *God*. Since we are bought and paid for by his blood, we have an obligation to glorify *God in our body and spirit 1 Corinthians 6:20*

Verse 7, also describes the *5ᵗʰ* blessing, *the forgiveness of sins.* It is closely related to redemption, but looks at the other side of the coin. In paying the ransom for our sins, the debt of sin was canceled and we were forgiven. We no longer have the burden of guilt for violating *God's* holy laws.

The *6ᵗʰ* blessing is knowing *his will* in *Ephesians 1:8–10 God* has given us wisdom and insight through his word and has shown us his desire to bring all things together to glorify *Christ.* Since all of creation was made by him and is for his good pleasure. *Revelation 4:11,* the consummation of his plan is when everything and everyone is brought in line to glorify Him.

By aligning ourselves with him by faith, we become part of his perfect plan and purpose. *"**But as it is written, Eye hath not seen, nor ear heard, neither have entered into the heart of man, the things which God hath prepared for them that love him" (KJV)**

1 Corinthians 2:9

Another *blessing* is found in *"Ephesians 1:13",* which is the sealing of the *Holy Spirit.* When we become *God's* children, He places His mark of ownership on us, guaranteeing our *eternal security.* This is spoken of as the down-payment of our *full redemption,* to hold us until the day *Christ* brings us to him.

➢ Those were the listing of the *"spiritual blessings"* that the *LORD* has given to the *Church* (*the body of Christ*).

The *LORD* also blesses in the *Natural;* with *good health, material goods & prosperity.* The *good health* blessing deal's with being *spiritually, physically, emotionally & mentally & financially well.* For *Isaiah 53:5*-says *"But he was wounded for our transgressions, he was bruised for our iniquities: the chastisement of our peace was upon him; and with his stripes we are healed"(KJV)*

➢ **(KJV) Psalm 35:27-"Let them shout for joy, and be glad, that favour my righteous cause: yea, let them**

say continually, Let the LORD be magnified, which hath pleasure in the prosperity of his servant."

- When *God* blesses, he does it so the human soul can prosper. Look at what he said in <u>*3 John 1:2*</u>-"*Beloved, I wish above all things that thou mayest prosper and be in health, even as thy soul prospereth." (KJV)*

The *LORD* wants you to be blessed beyond measure. That was his main goal through *Adam & Eve* to *bless humanity,* but because of their sin, that changed his agenda.

But *God restored* his original plan of blessings through *Jesus Christ.* Once you are connected to *Christ* by being *born again* through *spiritual new birth.* You will have access to receive *"God's spiritual & natural blessings".*

And when you are blessed by *God*, remember his favor will rest upon you.

For *Jesus Christ* is at the right hand of *God* making intercession for you, so you can be *bless.* <u>*You do not have to fear, the schemes & plots of the devil and his demons*</u>. Because, *"No weapons formed against you shall prosper, and every tongue which rises against you in judgment, the LORD will condemn".* ***This is the heritage of the servants of the LORD, and their righteousness is from Me," says the LORD.*** <u>***(KJV) Isaiah 54:17***</u>

When you are blessed of the *LORD* you don't have to worry because *God* will fight your battles for you, and he will give you the *victory.* And every schemes & plots of the enemy against you will back fire on them. *Remember God's blessings* on your life will always prevail against the attacks of the devil & his demons.

Look it how Israel as a nation were able to overcome pharaoh & his men in Egypt. *And also how they conquer the city of Jericho* to gain their *promise land.* The *Lord, God* will cause your enemies to be your footstool.

I'm telling you when *God blesses* you, doors will be open & good opportunities will come to you. You have to truly believe that you are *blessed* no matter what you go through. Obstacles & circumstances cannot prevent *God's blessings* to stop working in your life.

One of the signs of being bless is when you overcome the giants you face in your life. <u>Just like how</u>, David brought down goliath with a sling shot & a rock. The *sling shot* represents your *faith*, & the *rock* represents *Jesus Christ*. The *LORD's* blessing upon *King David's* life allowed him to gain the *victory*.

"Even by the God of thy father, who shall help thee; and by the Almighty, who shall bless thee with blessings of heaven above, blessings of the deep that lieth under, blessings of the breasts, and of the womb:" <u>(KJV)</u> <u>Genesis 49:25</u>

One of the ways to ignite *God's blessings* in your life is through obedience. When you are obedient unto the *LORD & his ways of living?* He will open up the windows of heaven & pour out tremendous blessings unto you.

<u>*Obedience unto God will cause blessings to chase & find you*</u>. What you need to realize is *God* has your best interest because he created you. He is a loving heavenly father who truly cares for his children and he wants the best for them.

Another way to unlock *God's blessings* in your life is by expressing love to others. When you love the *"LORD your God with your whole heart, soul, mind & strength, as well as, love your neighbor as yourself"*, God will bless you.

The *acronym* for "**<u>L.o.v.e</u>**", is "**<u>Living on victory everyday</u>**". Loving others will motivate *God to bless you*, because he is a *God of Love*. <u>That's what love does is provides ways for you to be bless.</u> *Every born again* believer who has accepted & received *Jesus Christ* as their *Savior and Lord*, are *blessed*. That's one of the benefits that comes with receiving <u>*Salvation*</u> & being <u>*SAVED*</u>.

The *Almighty God's* intention and desire to bless humanity is a central focus of his covenant relationships. For this reason, the concept of blessing pervades the biblical record. Two distinct ideas are presented. <u>*First*</u>, a *blessing was a public declaration of a favored status with God*. And <u>*Second*</u>, *the blessing endowed power for prosperity and success.* ***"The blessing of the Lord, it maketh rich, and he addeth no sorrow with it." (KJV) Proverbs 10:22***

In all cases, the blessing served as a guide and motivation to pursue a course of life within the blessing. *God* is in the business of blessing his children so he can have a *divine bless family* on earth. The *LORD* does not want to just keep the blessings to himself because he wants to share it. He is already *blessed*; so why not spread the *wealth of his blessings.*

Remember, *God* does not run out of blessings because he creates them. *Which means you do not need to hate on another person's success?* Always be happy when someone *gets bless*; because the *LORD* honors that. When you are happy for others, it will motivate the LORD to also bless you.

For you are a *"holy nation, a royal priesthood,* a *peculiar people"* unto the *LORD.* ***"Blessed is the nation whose God is the Lord; and the people whom he hath chosen for his own inheritance." (KJV) Psalm 33:12*** The *LORD* gets pleasure of blessing his people because it is our *rightful inheritance.*

He does not like to see you struggling or going through hardship, trying to make ends meet. He desires above all things that you prosper & be in health, just as your soul prospers. *He is the blesser that wants to bless you in all of the areas of your life.*

The LORD your *God* is a *blesser* who wants to give you the desires of your heart. For it is the father's good pleasure to give you the *Kingdom & its inheritance.* But you have to be willing to receive it by faith. *Selah!!!*

JEHOVAH-ROHI

Selah: 8

THE PROTECTOR

<u>**Definition:**</u> *A **Protector** is a person that protects & safeguards from danger.*

<u>**Synonym**</u>: *defender, preserver, guardian, champion, armor, guardian angel, patron, chaperone, escort, keeper, custodian, bodyguard, minder;*

<u>*(KJV) Psalm 9:1*</u>*-He that dwelleth in the secret place of the most High shall abide under the shadow of the Almighty.*

<u>*(KJV) 2 Thessalonians 3:3*</u>*-But the Lord is faithful, who shall stablish you, and keep you from evil.*

Besides of the other things that *God* specializes in; he is definitely efficient when it comes to *protection*. His by product name is *"JEHOVAH-ROHI"* the *LORD Shepherd,* who *guides & protects* his peoples.

The book of "<u>*Psalm 23*</u>" reminds us that "*the LORD is our Shepherd & He makes us to lie down in green pastures; He leads us beside the still waters, He restores our soul; He leads us in the path of righteousness, For his name sake. Even though we walk through the valley of shadow of death, we will fear no evil; For He is with us, His rod & staff, they comfort us. (NKJV)*

That's what a *shepherd* do, is safeguards his sheep from the attack of wolves". Throughout the *bible* there are many passages of *scriptures* that illustrate's *God's* protection for his children. Whether it was through <u>*his*</u>

Judges, his Prophets, his Kings & his Priests in the *Old Testament*? And in the *New Testament*, it was through his *Apostles & Servants*. The LORD always made a way to protect what belongs to him.

The *Lord Jesus Christ* is known as "*The Good Shepherd*" who gave his life for the sheep. The *Lord* will do whatever is necessary to make sure the sheep is well taken care of. Unlike some of these under shepherds who will *fleece* and leave their flock unprotected. The *LORD* is committed to caring for his people & for watching over them.

What we need to realize is we are the *LORD's treasure and his investment.* The *Body of Christ, the Church is the LORD's prize possession.* He will go to the extent to make sure that his *chosen & called out ones* the "*ekklesia*", aka the "*Church*" is safeguarded from danger. That's what a *Good Shepherd* do, is protect those that belongs to him.

A *loving father* does not only provide for his children but he also shields them. *God* is the same way; he will be there to keep you from harm's way. I know we are living in a world where there is recklessness & violence. But no need to be alarmed for the *LORD* will keep watch over you.

God has given his children access to him through prayer so they can be safe. *Prayer* is your source of communication with your *heavenly father*, so he can *cover you*. Always *pray* before you step out of the house for the LORD's guidance & protection. **The LORD is my light and my salvation; whom shall I fear? the LORD is the strength of my life; of whom shall I be afraid? When the wicked, even mine enemies and my foes, came upon me to eat up my flesh, they stumbled and fell. Though an host should encamp against me, my heart shall not fear: though war should rise against me, in this will I be confident. Psalm 27:1-3 (KJV)**

God is also known as "*JEHOVAH-SABAOTH*" the *LORD* of *hosts, & armies* who will fight your battles. Just like how he did for *Israel* in *Egypt*, & also in the wilderness. He will also do the same for you because he cares about you.

When it comes to *the LORD's safe keeping*, he will also protect you from the unwise decisions that you make. Some things he may allow, just so you can learn from it. And other things he will intervene to protect you from. His protection covers a wide range of things; such as *animals, plants, natural resources; & of course humanity.*

The *LORD* is *"EL-Elyon" the Most High God* who watches over the *Universe.* Nobody is hidden from *God's sight because he is Omniscient. God* is in control and he is aware of what's going on in the world. He is a *God of justice* who sits on the circle of the *Earth.* And who has all powers in his hand making decisions that will better the land. For his protection is not limited to just shielding your *physical embodiment,* but he also covers the other elements of your life, *spiritually, mentally, emotionally & financially.*

THE *GOOD* SHEPHERD

> **Here is a list** of the things that **the LORD Safeguards**.

God protects from *Danger-(KJV) (Psalm 91:1-3)*

God protects the *Poor-(KJV) (Psalm 14:6)*

God protects from *Temptation-(KJV) (1Corinthians 10:13)*

God protects from *Evil-(KJV) (Psalm 27 & (KJV) (2Thessalonians 3:3*

God protects from *Enemies-(KJV) (Deuteronomy 20:1-4)*

God protects from *Calamities-(KJV) (Psalm 57:1*

God protects his *Church-(KJV) (Matthew 16:18)*

God protects from *Persecution-(KJV) (Luke 21:18)*

> **God also provides protection for Spiritual warfare** through his armor. He has given you & I his *whole armor*, so we can withstand the wiles (*schemes*) of the devil.

(KJV) Ephesians 6:10-18-For we wrestle not against flesh and blood, but against principalities, against powers, against the rulers of the darkness of this world, against spiritual wickedness in high places. Wherefore take unto you the whole armour of God, that ye may be able to withstand in the evil day, and having done all, to stand. For we do not wrestle against flesh & blood, but against principalities, against powers, against the rulers of darkness of this age, against the spiritual forces of wickedness in the heavenly places. Therefore take up the whole armor of *God* that you may be able to withstand in the evil day, and having done all, to stand firm.

The Lord Provides his Whole Armor for spiritual warfare:

THE HELMET OF SALVATION-Helps you to stay believing that Jesus Christ died for your sins & that he rose again.

THE SHIELD OF FAITH-signifies your faith is being sure that God will keep His promises. Faith in God protects you when you are tempted to doubt.

THE BREASTPLATE OF RIGHTEOUSNESS-Righteousness is being honest, good, humble and fair to others by maintaining your integrity. It also means standing up for weaker people.

THE BELT OF TRUTH-Truth keeps us from giving in to the world's beliefs. Compare your beliefs and actions to the truth of the word of God.

THE SWORD OF THE SPIRIT- It is the word of God. God's word is our defense weapon. It protects us from the enemy (the devil & his demons). It also edify, especially when we tell others what the bible says, the Holy Spirit will help people see their bad thoughts and actions, and makes them want to be forgiven.

THE GOSPEL OF PEACE-Having shod your feet with the preparation of the Gospel of Peace. The Gospel of Peace is being right with God & being content in the midst of your trials. Jesus said that peace makers were blessed.

The *Lord's Armor* is his defense shield that he has provided for his *Children, his Servants & also for his Church (the Body of Christ)* against harmed. **Matthew 16:18**

God's protection is vast; it's not limited only in the *natural,* it also deals with the *spiritual. God* foresees the seen, & the unseen dangers. And he knows how to prevent you from being harmed by them. Just like how he told *Noah* to build an *Ark*, before the flood came about.

He prepared *Noah & his family* so they would be safe from the destruction of the flood. *Noah* obeyed *God* & he did what the *LORD* commanded him to do. <u>*Obedience* is also a form of protection that *God* uses to keep you safe.</u>

The *bible* said that *Noah* did what the *LORD* commanded him to do. And because of that his life, as well as his family lives were spared. *God* protected *Noah* because of his obedience to him. **<u>(KJV) Hebrews 3:15-</u> says, "While it is said, Today if ye will hear his voice, harden not your hearts, as in the provocation".**

God wants you to be receptive to <u>*hearing*</u> *&* <u>*obeying*</u> him. His instructions are always good for you because he can see around the corner before you get there. He is *"Omniscient-all knowing"* and *"Omnipresent-at all places at the same time".* He *see's* the *past, present & future* at the same time because he is *eternal.*

In *biblical times* the *LORD* provided *Israel* with protection through the *Ark of the Covenant.* The *Ark of the Covenant* symbolized *God's* <u>*presence*</u> *&* <u>*promise*</u>, which brought *protection & safety* to *Israel.* The point that I am making is the *LORD* can protect you whichever way he choose *too.*

He can use whatever source of channel to provide protection for his *creation.* Just like how he died on the *Cross* at *Calvary,* so you and I can receive *deliverance.* He used a *cross* to bring *salvation* to *humanity. Jesus Christ* was *God's vessel* that he used to provide safety for humanity from their sins. He is *"EMMANUEL" "God is with us",* and he will keep us from the snare of the fowler.

Eternal life is also a form of protection from the damnation of hell. *Eternal life* starts on *Earth* and it continues in *Heaven. Our heavenly father* gave us *eternal life* through *Christ,* so we can be *set free* from destruction. *OH! Praise be to GOD!!!*

God has given you *"66 Books"* to inspire & edify you. The *Holy Bible* is *God's* way of keeping you safe from the ignorance of this *world system. God's word is a lamp unto your feet & a light unto your path that will guide you and keep you safe. Jesus Christ* is the living word which provides *stability & safety.*

The *Holy Scriptures* were written to keep you safe from the ignorance of darkness. The *LORD* wants you to be wise, *"In all thy getting, get an understanding"*. *Christ* is the wisdom of *God* & he illuminates you through his *word,* so you can walk in *righteousness.* The Almighty *God* gave us the Holy Bible to *inform, inspire, encourage* & to *edify* us-**"All Scripture is given by inspiration of God, and is profitable for doctrine, for reproof, for correction, for instruction in righteousness"-2 Timothy 3:16 (KJV)**

The *word of God* will also protect you from *false doctrines* and *heresies.* God's word is infallible because it was written under the guidance of the Holy Spirit & his spirit will guide you in all truth.

Here is a list of the things that the **_word of God_** *protects* you from:

- *God's word protects you from Error*

- *God's word protects you from Ignorance*

- *God's word protects you from Disobedience*

- *God's word protects you from Sin*

- *God's word protects you from Apostasy*

- *God's word protects you from Confusion*

- *God's word protects you from Doubt*

- *God's word protects you from Worry*

Jesus Christ; the *"Prince of Peace"* will also protect you from anything that will disrupt your *peace of mind.* Whether it be; *stress, anxiety, frustration, depression, aggravation, oppression, disappointment, or fear.* You don't need a bottle of *alcohol, or illegal drugs* to give you *peace & fulfillment.* Just rely on *Jesus Christ* & he will give you peace from your troubles. ***"Come unto me, all ye that labour and are heavy laden, and I will give you rest" (KJV) Matthew 11:28***

The *Almighty Creator* wants to make sure that you are *safe* in every *area of your life.* The LORD is your *Ark* that will carry you through the storms of life; so you can make it on shore *safely.* Life is full of twist & turns, but no need to be alarmed because *Jesus Christ is your life saver.* He will rebuke the wind & then calm the storms in your life, *just so you can be at peace.* ***"And he arose, and rebuked the wind, and said unto the sea, Peace, be still. And the wind ceased, and there was a great calm." (KJV) Mark 4:39***

"YAHWEH THE GREAT" will *sustain & keep you* from the onslaught of the enemy's devices. *He will protect you & fight your battles, so you can get the victory, as well as the last laugh!!! Thanks be to GOD!!!*

TRUE & LIVING "GOD"

Selah: 9

THE LIFE GIVER

Life is an expedition, & we are here on earth to experience it. Besides you being here to live out your *purpose*; life is also a gift to *enjoy*. Too many of us focus so much on the purpose part of our lives, that we neglect the *journey of it*. For some reason we either reflect more on our *past* or we focus too much on our *future*. It's rarely that you see people enjoy their *present* moments. We are living in an era where everyone seems to be in a hurry, always rushing. It's either *seek success* or be *purpose driven*. And because of that we forget to enjoy the *gift of life*.

Society has forgotten the simplicity of life living of just being happy. I feel like the scale is weighting more towards on the demands of life; *instead of just living it*.

"Now", don't get me wrong I know people have to work to make a *living*. As well as, fulfill their *purpose*, & live out their *dreams*. But if you focus on those things too much with no balance, you can end up missing the precious moments. The *bible* says that life is like a *vapor*, in others it's like a *Kodak moment*-(A *Quick flash*). *And If you don't catch it; then you'll miss it.*

God created this earth so human beings can explore it. You will be surprise to know the people who are frustrated & unhappy because of the lack of balance in their lives. All they do is work to pay bills, without making the time to *"vacay and play"*.

Some people are *alive,* & others are *living.* <u>Don't you know that you can</u> <u>be *alive*-but not be *living.*</u> There is a difference with being alive, & living. To be alive is to just exist & to live is to be conscious of every moment that you encounter. The *LORD* gave you life for a reason. For a healthy life, is a well balanced life. *God* did not create you to be *a robot & to live stress out.* The *LORD* came to give you life with more abundance. And that abundance comes with *joy and happiness.*

When I say living; I'm not talking about just working to pay bills. But enjoying the fact that you are alive, so you can witness the beauty of *life?* You will be surprise to know the amount of people who contemplates on committing suicide because they are not happy with their lives.

And if you are one of those people that is reading this book right now, here is an encouragement to you. *"Don't give in, don't breakdown & don't give up",* "*for weeping may endure for a night, but joy will come in the morning".* *And also "the joy of the LORD is your strength".* You can lean on *God* and give him your *anxieties,* your *d*epression, your *disappointments, your frustrations, your aggravations* & also your *personal challenges.* So *cast your cares upon the LORD because he can handle it.*

Remember, *God* is your *life giver* who will help you to be at ease. No need to commit suicide or to give up on life. If *God* gave you life then he can also *sustain* & help you *through it.*

The *LORD* is the *"EL-SHADDAI";* the *All-Sufficient* one, who is your *supporter and comforter.* At times you may feel like your back is up against the wall, but give *God* a chance. *And watch him work it out for you. The LORD* will *refreshen* your *soul,* and he will uplift your *spirit.* The *Lord* is the *prince of life,* who *sustains life.* "*So don't give up on God, cause he won't give up on you,* "*because he's able".*

The *LORD* is your anchor who will uphold you in times of trouble. So don't lose heart and don't lose hope. Once again, he is your life giver and sustainer; *who's* got you in the *palm of his hand.* <u>*Selah!!!*</u>

THE GLORY CARRIER

"*Glory*" is one of the most common word in *the bible*. In the *Old Testament*, the word is used to translate several *Hebrew* words, including "*Hod*" and "*kabod*". And in the *New Testament* it is used to translate the *Greek* word "*doxa*".

The word "*Kabod*" means, "*Glory*" which denotes *weight or heaviness*. The word "*kabod*" is a title for *God* that displays his "*Awesomeness*". The *Greek* word "*doxa*" is used for the *nature & acts of God*. It also stems from the word *doxology*, which means singing praises unto *God*. The book of *Psalms* is known as *doxology*, aka praises unto the *LORD*. "*Doxa*" signifies *God's* manifestation of his power. "*Kabod*" also illustrates *God's* weight of *power & action*.

As an example when the *LORD* delivered *Israel* out of *Egypt* from the opening of the *Red sea*. That was the *kabod* of *God*, which was the weight of his almighty hand acting on the behalf of his peoples. *God* likes to demonstrate his power through his glory.

For glory is the excellency of the *LORD's* might. *It* also exemplifies the *LORD's* sufficiency as the "*EL-Shaddai*" who is complete within himself. He is *three persons in one*, but equally the same as the *Holy Trinity*.

For the glory of *God* was seen in the character & the acts of *Christ*; as well as in the *Holy Spirit*. For the *almighty God* manifested his glory through the working of miracles in *Jesus*. The *Thirty-five plus miracles* that *Christ* performed in the *New Testament* were *God's* glory in action. *Whether it was the raising of the dead, or the healing of the sick, or power over nature? All were God's glory being manifested.*

This beginning of signs Jesus did in Cana of Galilee, and manifested His glory; and His disciples believed in Him. (KJV) John 2:11

Also the *Mount of Transfiguration* of the appearing of *Moses and Elijah* were the demonstration of *God's glory*. The ascension & exaltation of *Jesus Christ* was also the "*doxa*" and the "*kabod*" of *God* in demonstration.

In the life of a believer whenever *God* show himself *mighty & strong* that represents his *glory*. Which is the reason why when the *LORD* performs a miracle; we say *"Glory be to God"*? That is our expression of saying; *God did it and made it happen.*

The almighty God exemplifies his *glory* through *Jesus Christ* to work on your behalf. Since *Christ* is our mediator, *God* works through him to express his *glory*. **Jesus** said: **"Verily, verily, I say unto you, The Son can do nothing of himself, but what he seeth the Father do: for what things soever he doeth, these also doeth the Son likewise". (KJV) John 5:19**

Glory is also a *divine quality* that deals with the *splendor, brightness & radiance* of God's presence. It is *the LORD's* visible revelation of himself. *Jesus Christ* demonstrates the *personality, presence, and character* of the *almighty God*. *Christ* made the *glory* of *God* forever visible through *himself and his church.*

The *LORD* wants his *children* to carry out his *glory* by the things that we do. We are the *Lord's* representatives on planet earth. *"We are his hands, his feet, his heart & his mouth piece"*. *Which* is why the *church is his body* & *he* is the *head of it"*.

The only *Jesus* people will see is through you; by the way you *live & carry yourself*. *God's children* were placed on the earth, so people can witness his *glory*. In other words we are here to make *God look good*. "**Let your light so**

shine before men, that they may see your good works and glorify your Father in heaven". *(KJV) Matthew 5:16*

Our heavenly father wants us to let our light shine by making the effort to do good deeds, to live right, & by spreading the Gospel of Christ. God is the product; & the product is his glory that he manifests through the life of those who belongs to him. It is *our duty* to make a difference in the world. The *LORD* is looking for *glory carriers* that will *"let their light shine before others".* God wants to demonstrate his *"Shekinah" dwelling glory* in the midst of his *peoples. "All glory belongs to God".* He gets the credit for the manifestation of his work that he displays on your behalf. But he will bless you for being a *willing vessel* that he works through. The *"Kabod" of God* will touch many lives so his kingdom can be expanded on the earth. His *doxology* will motivate humanity to give him *"praise & worship"* because of his *splendor & his awesomeness.*

So once again, glory is a divine quality that deals with the *splendor, brightness & radiance* of *God's presence.* It is the *LORD's* visible revelation of himself. *Jesus Christ* demonstrates the *personality, presence, & character* of the almighty *God. Christ* made the *glory of God* forever visible through *himself and his church.* **"Moreover whom he did predestinate, them he also called: and whom he called, them he also justified: and whom he justified, them he also glorified. *(KJV) Romans 8:30* *(Amen!)*

Selah: 11

THE SUSTAINER

Definition: Sustainer is a person who sustains & upkeeps; as well as maintain in a supportive manner.

(KJV) 1 Kings 17:9 Arise, go to Zarephath, which belongs to Sidon, and dwell there. See, I have commanded a widow there to sustain you.

(KJV) Nehemiah 9:21-Forty years You sustained them in the wilderness; They lacked nothing; Their clothes did not wear out And their feet did not swell.

The Universe cannot function or maintain its course without *God's assistance*. Everything within the *Cosmos*; whether it's the *sun, moon & stars* has been set in place by the *Almighty Creator*. *God* has the power to call things into *existence* & he also has the ability to *sustain it*.

At times, *God* is only viewed as just the *Creator*. For some reason people neglect the fact that *God* is in control. Some people think that the *LORD* just sits back & just watch things happen in the universe. Which is not the case, the *LORD* is very aware with what's going on in our *World*. He may not respond to every situation, but trust me he is well aware of what's going on.

For his *ways & thoughts* is not like ours. But he see's and knows everything that's happening. When it's necessary then he steps in. Without his involvement the universe would not be able to propel on its axis. *Remember*

God is *all powerful*; as well as *intelligent*. He <u>creates</u>, <u>calculates</u>, <u>arranges</u> & <u>sustains</u> planet earth.

No one can live outside of *God*. If he did not want you to exist then you wouldn't be here. If he allowed it, then it's all part of his plan. *God* is a generous *Creator* who is mindful about his *Creation*.

<u>As an example</u>; whenever I go to the park I usually see someone feeding the *pigeons & the squirrels*. The *Almighty God* provides & sustains for his creation through people.

The *LORD* knows how to sustain what belongs to him. I remember when I was homeless back in *2002*. The *LORD* always made provision for me to eat throughout my day. He would give me ideas on what to do in order for me to survive on the streets of *New York City*. He would lead me to talk to certain people who would provide for me, just so I can *eat & survive*.

*E*ven throughout that experience he sustained me and eventually brought me out to *green pastures*. At times life can get quite challenging & you may say to yourself, how am I going to make it? Have no worries, *just trust God* & watch him make a way for you. Never view your problems to be bigger than *God*. In other words; don't tell *God* how big your problems are, but tell your problems how big your *God* is.

If the *LORD* can sustain the universe; then certainly he can uphold you. He did not bring you this far to leave you where you are. He will continue to make ways for you; as long you believe and act upon. *"If there is a will, then there is a way"*.

*E*very day you wake up in the morning is truly a blessing & a gift from *God*. He has sustained you with his *breath of life*. He has kept you alive, which determines the fact you still have purpose to fulfill? *The LORD* will sustain you & he will give you strength to persevere. He will find ways to encourage you when you feel like giving up. *God* cares about you. He is not oblivious to your problems or situations. He is well aware of what's going on in your life.

Food, clothes and *shelter* is *God's* way of sustaining his *creation*. It may not always be the things that you want but he knows how to give you the things that you need. The necessities of *food, clothes, shelter, health & finances; are* essential tools that are needed in order to survive and live on this earth.

Without food it would be difficult to do your daily activities. When I say food; I'm talking about *nutritious foods* that are good for you. *Such as* *water, grains, rice, vegetables, & fruits that comes straight from the ground.* Genesis 1:11-13 The LORD initiated and knew that natural food would be good for his *creation*, which is the reason why he planted them in the *ground of the earth?* So we can eat them to maintain a *healthy living. Good food* gives us the proper nutrients to keep us *fit & alive, so we can function on the earth.*

Clothes is also an important tool for a human being, because you cannot roam in public naked; this is not the *garden of Eden*. Wearing the proper clothes will also keep you warm from getting sick. *God* knew that the body would need attire to be able to operate in public, to keep you from being *indecency* exposed.

Another sustenance that our *Creator* uses to sustain us is *Shelter*. Everyone needs a roof over their head and a place to stay. You need a place that you can call your home. A place where you can take showers to be clean, a place where you can cook your food, a place where you can rest & get some sleep. Your home should be your *safe haven* because you spend more time there than any other place. *God* is smart and he already knew that his *creation* would need *habitation*.

Wandering in the streets is not good for your *soul & spirit*. You need a home where you can relax & chill; *meditate and pray*. The LORD also uses your home to be your place of covering from harm and danger. That's why it's called *shelter* because it covers you and keeps you *safe*.

Health is a very important factor because without it, you cannot *stay alive. Good health* is the key to *longevity*. Taking care of yourself through *health fitness, exercising, & proper eating* are very important. *God* uses *natural healing*, as well as *supernatural healing* to sustain the *body*.

God can heal you through a *doctor,* or he can do it *miraculously.* Your health is also your wealth. Without it; it would be impossible to live. The *LORD* will sustain you through your health so you can maintain your *being.*

Last but not least, God sustains through *Finances.* When it comes to money, certain people have a nonchalant attitude about it. People usually misinterpret the scripture when it comes with dealing with money. They say money is the root of evil*, which is incorrect. "For the love of money is the root of all evil", which is the correct scripture. (KJV) 1 Timothy 6:10*

Certain individual's think that money is evil, but it's not the money itself. It's what you do to acquire it. There is nothing wrong with liking & having money because you need it in order to survive. *It's how you obtain it.* If you do wrong things; like harming others to get it, then it becomes a problem.

But if you do the right things to acquire it, then *it's alright. God* will sustain you financially through the opportunity of a *job. Or he can bless you through your talents,* so you can obtain *money. D*espite what others may say; you need money to survive-*That's just the bottom line.* You cannot make it in this society without money, whether it's in the format of *cash or credit.* "*YOU NEED it!*"

You will be surprise to know that, one of the main factors that cause's stress & anxiety is the lack of *finances.* Which can lead to health issues, especially when you can't pay your bills? I believe that the *LORD* wants you to have more than enough, so you can live *comfortably. "He wants you to be in health, just as your soul prospers".*

Your soul prospering deals with the totality of you're being; *spiritually, mentally, emotionally, physically & financially.* Your heavenly father is a *God* of *sustenance* who provides you with the necessities so you can survive and make it on planet earth. He created and then sustains to preserve you. He is a *God* of purpose who makes *provisions.* No need to be alarm, just have faith & trust the *LORD. And watch all of your needs be applied for.*

JEHOVAH-RAPHA

Selah: 12

THE HEALER

Definition-A **_Healer_** _is a person that heals and that restores back to its proper condition or state of well being._

(KJV) Numbers 12:13-And Moses cried unto the LORD, _saying, Heal her now, O God, I beseech thee._

(KJV) 2 Chronicles 7:14-If my people, which are called by my name, shall humble themselves, and pray, and seek my face, and turn from their wicked ways; then will I hear from heaven, and will forgive their sin, and will heal their land.

Out of the _35 miracles Jesus Christ_ performed in the _Holy bible. 23_ of them were based on the _miraculous act of healing._ Beside the _LORD being a Creator, a Provider, a Way maker;_ he is also a _Healer._ In the _New Testament_ the _Lord_ is known as the _"Great Physician"_ & in the _Old Testament_ he is described as _"JEHOVAH-RAPHA",_ The _LORD that heals._

God specializes in _healing,_ and making people to be _whole._ He heals _spiritually, physically, emotionally, mentally & financially. God_ can heal you in every area of your life. The _LORD_ is well rounded and he has the cure to restore you back to health.

_He_ is the _Creator_ of all who knows every details within the _human body._ The _LORD_ is the one who formed man out of the dust of the ground, so

75

man can become a *living soul.* He created the human being, as a three part entity. Which is the *body,* the *spirit* & the *soul?* Each entity has its own function. The body is the compartment that houses the *spirit & soul.* The *spirit* gives the body *vitality,* & the *soul* displays the *will, intellect & emotion* of a person. ***"And the LORD God formed man of the dust of the ground, and breathed into his nostrils the breath of life; and man became a living soul." (KJV) Genesis 2:7***

The *almighty* is the *manufacturer,* as well as the *distributor* of life. He knows how to fix your *anatomy* because he is the one who created you. *God* can *heal,* & *restore* you, whichever way he chooses too. He can do it through his *miraculous healing power,* or through the *vehicle of a doctor & medicine.*

The *Lord* can spit on the ground, & make a mud pie. *And then rub it on your eyes to heal you.* He can also have you dip in water *seven times,* just like he did with *"Naaman",* so you can be healed. *2 Kings 5 & John 9:6*

Nothing is beyond *God's* reach when it comes to *healing you.* Whether you are dealing with sickness of the *mind, body & soul?* It doesn't matter; the *LORD* can restore you back to health. *All you got to do is trust, believe & watch him do it.*

*E*ven when we participate in *"Holy Communion",* partaking in the *Lord's body* & of his *blood?* He provides us with *healing and restoration* through it. As a *child of God* through *Jesus Christ* you have access to be *healed* & to be made *whole.* Because of the sacrifice *Jesus* made on the *cross of Calvary* for you. ***But he was wounded for our transgressions, he was bruised for our iniquities: the chastisement of our peace was upon him; and with his stripes we are healed." (KJV) Isaiah 53:5***

The *LORD* wants you to be made well *in mind, body & soul.* He takes delight in seeing his children to be *whole.* The LORD wants you to be *healed* from *stress, depression, anxiety & frustration* that comes with the challenges of life. *God loves you* and he wants you to be well in every area of your being.

Spiritually he wants you to be healthy so your relationship with him can blossom. I believe in some cases when you are *spiritually fit,* then it will propel your *physical body* to also be healed. *Remember* when *Jesus* healed the paralytic man & then he said your sins are forgiven. **"And, behold, they brought to him a man sick of the palsy, lying on a bed: and Jesus seeing their faith said unto the sick of the palsy; Son, be of good cheer; thy sins be forgiven thee."(<u>KJV</u>) <u>Matthew 9:2</u>**

> ➤ This particular *healing of* the paralytic man was based on his *spiritual condition. His sins had to be forgiven in order for him to be healed physically.*

Remember we are *spirit beings* housed in a *physical body. Jesus* wants your spirit person to be *well also, not just your physical.* Being & staying *connected* to the *"True vine"* will help you to be *spiritually* stable. *Jesus* is the vine and we are his branches. Staying connected to the *Lord* will cause you to receive your *spiritual nutrients.* That will *enable you* to *bear <u>fruit, more fruit</u> & <u>much fruit</u>.*

Beside your *spirit person, God* also created your physical body so you can live on the earth. Being *physically healthy* is very important to *God* because he wants you to live a *fulfilling life.* Without you being physically healthy, how can you fulfill your purpose. Your health is also your wealth. You need it so you can function to get things done.

<u>*Like I stated earlier in the previous chapter*</u>; lack of finances can also cause distress, which is not good for your *mind, body & soul.* You will be surprise to know people who are stress because of the lack of finances. Not being able to put food on the table, or to pay their bills. It's not a good feeling when you are *malnutritious* in your finances. The *LORD* wants your pockets to be fat-"<u>*literally*</u>", so you can be healthy financially also.

Financial hardship can also cause frustrations that can lead to worry & then stress. And once stress comes into play it can cause sickness within the body. Health in the human life deals with wholeness in ones being. It covers all areas within your life. *Jesus* came to give you life with more abundance.

Which is why whatever you lack, *God* can make up the difference? *"By supplying all of your needs according to his riches & glory"!!!*

> ### Here is a list of the people in the Holy Scriptures who were financially healthy.

The *Patriarchs* of the *Old Testament* were very rich and prosperous. According to *Acts 10:34* and *Romans 2:11*,

God is no respecter of persons. This means God does not show partiality. What he did for the patriarchs he will also do for you. As long you operate in faith & apply his principles then watch God make a way for you.

Abraham Through a personal relationship with Jesus, according to *(KJV) Galatians 3:14*, Jesus made the blessings of Abraham available to anyone that will have them. Abraham was an extremely rich, successful and prosperous man!

And Abram was very rich in cattle, in silver, and in gold. *(KJV) Genesis 13:2*

Isaac Then Isaac sowed in that land, and received in the same year an hundredfold: and the LORD blessed him. And the man waxed great, and went forward, and grew until he became very great: For he had possession of flocks, and possession of herds, and great store of servants: and the Philistines envied him. *(KJV) Genesis 26:12-14*

Jacob And Esau took his wives, and his sons, and his daughters, and all the persons of his house, and his cattle, and all his beasts, and all his substance, which he had got in the land of Canaan; and went into the country from the face of his brother Jacob. For their riches were more than that they might dwell together; and the land wherein they were strangers could not bear them because of their cattle. *(KJV) Genesis 36:6-7*

King David And he died in a good old age, full of days, riches, and honour: and Solomon his son reigned in his stead. *(KJV) 1 Chronicles 29:28*

King David stated, I have been young, and now am old; yet have I not seen the righteous forsaken, nor his seed begging bread *(KJV) Psalms 37:25*

<u>Solomon</u> And King Solomon passed all the kings of the earth in riches and wisdom *(KJV) 2 Chronicles 9:22*

<u>Jehoshaphat</u> Therefore the LORD established the kingdom in his hand; and all Judah brought to Jehoshaphat presents; and he had riches and honour in abundance. *(KJV) 2 Chronicles 17:5*

<u>Hezekiah</u> Notwithstanding Hezekiah humbled himself for the pride of his heart, both he and the inhabitants of Jerusalem, so that the wrath of the LORD came not upon them in the days of Hezekiah. And Hezekiah had exceeding much riches and honour: and he made himself treasuries for silver, and for gold, and for precious stones, and for spices, and for shields, and for all manner of pleasant jewels; Storehouses also for the increase of corn, and wine, and oil; and stalls for all manner of beasts, and cotes for flocks. *(KJV) 2 Chronicles 32:26-28*

<u>Joseph of Arimathaea</u> When the even was come, there came a rich man of Arimathaea, named Joseph, who also himself was Jesus' *(KJV) Matthew 27:57*

So if the LORD can do it for these *biblical figures,* then *"Guess what"* he can also do it for you. *Just believe & trust him. "And he will heal your finances by opening up the windows of heaven, & by pouring out his financial blessings upon you".* The *LORD* wants you to be healed in every aspect of your life. *Spiritually, physically, emotionally, mentally & especially, financially.* He is able to do it for you because he is *"Jehovah Rapha"* the *LORD* that heals.

Healing does play a big part of that abundant life because it will keep you intact so you can function well. The *Almighty God* is your *healer* and he has the cure for the problems that arises in one's life. *He will prescribe you with the proper medication to help make you feel better.* **"Heal me, O LORD, and I shall be healed; save me, and I shall be saved: for thou art my praise. (KJV) Jeremiah 17:14**

JESUS SAVES!!!

Selah: 13

THE REDEEMER

Definition: "**Redeem**" *means to compensate for the faults or bad aspects of (something). To regain possession in exchange for payment.*

Redeemer *is a person that redeems someone or something from danger or error. The theological term for redeemer is a person that buys back or pays for the freedom of an individual.*

(KJV) Titus 2:14-To redeem them that were under the law, that we might receive the adoption of sons.

Redemption is the synonym for the word *Salvation*; which means to be *saved, set free & delivered*. Redemption is the action of saving or being saved from sin, error, or evil. It is the action of regaining the possession of something in exchange for payment to clear a debt. It is the purchase of something that was lost, by the payment of a ransom.

The *Greek word* for *redemption* is *"apolutrosis"*, which occurs nine times in the scriptures, and it is the idea of a ransom, or price paid for. It means *release* or *deliverance* from harm, danger and from negative consequences.

The concept of redemption deals with the forgiveness of sins. There are many passages of scriptures in the *New Testament,* which represents *Christ* sufferings under the idea of *ransom. God* made the payment through the sacrificial offering of his son *Jesus Christ* to redeem humanity.

The debt's from our sins is not only viewed as cancelled, but it has been fully paid. *Christ blood paid* our debts that we could not pay for ourselves. It was and it is still *God's* plans for the redemption of this world through *Jesus Christ. 2 Peter 3:9*

The concept of *redemption* was always in effect even in the "*Old Testament*". The *High Priest* would go into the *Tabernacle* once a year to make atonements for his sins, & *also for the sins of the people of Israel? Hebrews 9:7*

The *High Priest* and his assistants would go into the *Tabernacle* to offer up different types of animals for sacrifices such as *bulls, sheep, goats & birds.* Based on the different type of sins they would offer up unto the *LORD* for the remission of their sins. *Leviticus Chapter 16*

➢ *Here is a list of scriptures in the Old Testament for the different type of Sacrificial Offerings:*

- *Burnt Offering*-A sacrifice made for complete dedication & surrender to *God. Leviticus 1:1-17*

- *Grain or Meal Offering*-A sacrifice made to express thanksgiving to *God. Leviticus 2:1-16*

- *Peace Offering*-A sacrifice made to fellowship & to be at peace with *God. Leviticus 3:1-17*

- *Sin Offering*-A sacrifice made to feel sorry or to be guiltless for one's sin. *Leviticus 4:1-35*

- *Trespass Offering*-A sacrifice made to express forgiveness of one's violation against another. *Leviticus 5 & 6*

The Day of "*Atonement*" is also known as "*Yom Kippur*" which is the most solemn holy day for the Jewish people. *Yom* means (day) & *Kippur* means (atonement or covering). Atonement means the reconciliation of *God* & human beings; to bring back into a right relationship.

Before the fall of man which dealt with the *"Original sin"* of *Adam & Eve*. We were in right standing with *God our Creator*. But because of the disobedience of *Adam & Eve*, we had lost that right standing relationship with the *LORD*. So *God* in his infinite wisdom provided a way for human beings to be reconciled back to him through the sacrifice of *atonement*.

The *High Priest* at that time was *"Aaron"* the brother of *"Moses"*. Aaron would go into the *Tabernacle* to offer up sacrifice unto *God* on the behalf of himself & *Israel*.

> ➤ *Footnote*: The *"Prophet"* spoke on the behalf of *God* & the *"Priest"* spoke on the behalf of *God's peoples*.

When the *High Priest* was finished making atonement for his sins & also for the sins of the people; a goat was released into the wilderness, as a *"scape goat"*. The *scape goat* represented the carrying of the sins of *Israel*, never to return.

Leviticus 16:8-10 & 20-22 & 29-34-The *Tabernacle* was a moveable tent of meeting for *God* & the people of *Israel*. *God* commanded *Moses* to build it because the *LORD* wanted to dwell among his people, the *Israelites*. He wanted to have fellowship with them, and to be able to communicate with them.

The *Tabernacle* was set up like a temple but it was out doors. The *Tabernacle* and its courtyard were constructed according to a pattern set by *God*, not by *Moses*. The *Tabernacle* was built around *"1440 BC"*, and it was the center of *Israelites camp*. The *12 tribes of Israel* camped around in a special arrangement in the direction of *East-West & North-South*.

It was in the *Tabernacle* that these animal offerings were made up to the LORD for the redemption of the sins of the people of Israel. Years later these offerings were presented in the *Temple* instead of the *Tabernacle* during the time of *King Solomon's* reign. *Redemption* is of *God* & it's by *Christ*. *In other words* God initiated it & *Jesus Christ* activated it.

*T*he concept of redemption in the *Old Testament* was a *"typology"* of *Christ* redemption in the *New Testament*. The *New Testament* is concealed in the *Old Testament,* and the *Old Testament* is revealed in the *New Testament*. *Jesus* was the *sacrificial lamb who's blood* was *shed & smeared* on the *door posts* of *Israel* in *Egypt*. The *blood* signified *redemption of deliverance*. The *blood of Christ* has *lasting power* because it's *efficacious*, it *prevails*, *sets free* & *delivers*.

Jesus is the *epitome* of *redemption* because of what he did over *2000 years ago* on the *cross at Calvary*. His sacrifice still resonates till this day, & nobody can redeem you except *Jesus Christ*. No other religious god has done such a thing. **"Neither is there salvation in any other: for there is none other name under heaven given among men, whereby we must be saved." (KJV) Acts 4:12 (Hosanna! Hosanna! Hosanna!)**

The *Almighty God* through his son *Jesus Christ* made it possible for you to receive *salvation* because of what he did on the *cross*.

*The Acronym for "**C.R.O.S.S**" is*

(**C**rowned Jesus with Glory)-

(**R**edeemed us back to God)-

(**O**vercame the World)-

(**S**aved from the consequence of sin)-

(**S**hed blood for the remissions of our sins)

The *bible* says, *"live out your own salvation with fear & trembling"*, in other words workout your redemption by honoring it because of its value. You will be surprise to know of those who are *redeem & saved*. But who has no clue about their *redemption spiritual package plan. Your redemption* is not only something that you work out but it is a gift that comes from *GOD* to every believer.

Redemption also denotes "*Grace being applied to our lives*". *Ephesians 2, v8-* says "*you have been saved by Grace through Faith & not of yourself, but it is a gift from GOD; & you cannot brag about it.*

Redemption is like a tree that has many branches attached too it. In other words your *redemption* is the tree; & the branches from the tree are the benefit's that comes from being *redeemed. Redemption* is the base of your faith walk in the *Lord.* It transforms the nature of your being for the better. The *Almighty God* used *Jesus* to *redeem you* to *himself. For Christ stated in John 14:6, that he is the way, the truth, and the life: no man cometh unto the Father, but by me". (KJV)*

The *Acronym* for "***J.E.S.U.S***" is

(***J**ustified*)

(***E**ternal life giver*)

(***S**alvation restorer*)

(***U**ndeniable truth*)

(***S**in forgiver & Redeemer*)

It is very important as a believer to know the benefits that comes with your *redemption.* Just like a working job that offers certain benefit packages, whether it be for *health, dental coverage, or (401k) financial residuals.* You as a born again, *child of God* also have spiritual *benefit's* that comes with being *redeemed & saved.*

> ➢ *The Benefits of redemption includes,*

1. *Eternal life (Revelation 5:9-10)*

2. *Forgiveness of sins (Ephesians 1:7)*

3. *Righteousness being Justified (Romans 5:17),*

4. *Freedom from the law's curse (Galatians 3:13)*

5. *Adoption into God's family (Galatians 4:5)*

6. *Deliverance from sin's bondage (Titus 2:14; 1 Peter 1:14-18)*

7. *Peace with God (Colossians 1:18-20)*

8. *The indwelling of the Holy Spirit (1 Corinthians 6:19-20)*

• Once you become born again by accepting *Jesus Christ* as your *Savior*, then the process of your benefits begins to take place.

➢ **Here is a list of the other *benefits* that comes with being *saved* by receiving the gift of *redemption* through *Jesus Christ*.**

Regeneration; is a spiritual birth that takes place as the form of being *born again,* which is the renewal of the *spirit*. It is *God's* transformation in the life of the believer. It is also the act of turning from one's sin in repentance and turning to *Christ in faith.*

Regeneration provides access to the *body of Christ (the Church)* into *God's* spiritual family. It is also intertwined with the baptism of the water & of the *Holy Spirit*. Because of this process of being "*Born Again*" you can now partake into fellowship with the *God head* of the *Holy Trinity*; which is the *Father, the Son & the Holy Ghost.* Once you receive *redemption* by accepting *Jesus Christ.* You will be given access to become part of the *(Kingdom of GOD & HEAVEN); as well as in the sacraments* of the *Church. John 3:1-7 & Romans 8:17*

Adoption-In the *Greek l*anguage is the word "*huiothesia*" or "*huios*" meaning *Son.* It is a legal term that indicates that believers have been given the full privilege of *Sonship* in *God's family.* In the *Sonship* there is no gender; there is no distinction between *a man or a woman. Galatians 3:28 (neither male nor female; for you are all one in Christ Jesus (KJV)* For this placement into *Sonship*; *God* will place the spirit of *Jesus Christ* in your heart so that you can become *effective*, as his *spiritual born children*.

The nature of "*Sonship*" of your *adoption* occurs once you become *born again, in receiving Jesus Christ*. Even though *adoption* is reasonably detectable from *regeneration and justification*, the concept is not divisible from each other.

Adoption is the recipient of *God's* fatherly care. In other words, *God* will *take care, protect*; as well as *provide* for you because of the benefit of *adoption*. You will have *kingdom privileges*; as being *Abraham seed* & a partaker of his *blessings*.

You will also have the access to come boldly to the throne of *God's grace*, claiming that you are his *son or daughter*. **"Having predestinated us unto the adoption of children by Jesus Christ to himself, according to the good pleasure of his will" (KJV) Ephesians 1:5**

Sanctification in the *Greek language* is the word "*qadash*", which is to be *made holy*. *Sanctification* is the process where *God* develops & makes the new life of the believer to become *holy*. It is the method by which ones moral condition is brought into conformity with ones legal status before GOD. During the process of *sanctification* there are "*instant sanctification*" and "*progressive sanctification*".

For "*instant sanctification*" deals with the *spirit* which takes place during the *conversion* stage of being *born again*. "*Progressive sanctification*" deals with the *soul*, which is a lifelong process of being conformed into the *image of Christ*. **"For whom He foreknew, he also predestinated them to be conformed to the image of his dear Son. Romans 8:29 (KJV)**

Sanctification co-relates with *conversion* because it deals with the transformation of the *heart & spirit*. It is *Gods* transformation of an individual by giving them a new *spiritual birth*. *Conversion* deals with a *repentance heart & attitude* that stems from *redemption*.

Propitiation in the *Greek language* is the word *"hilasterion"* meaning *to win or to regain favor* of, & it deals with *substitution*. It is *Christ* substituting his life for yours by paying the price for your sins. He gave his life; so you can have *new life through Him*. Like the saying goes, *"He died to save you & He lives to keep you"*.

For *Jesus* paid the consequences & punishment for your sins. He made it possible through *propitiation*. **"For the wages of sin is death but the gift of God is eternal life through Jesus Christ our Lord" (KJV) Romans 6:23**

Because of *propitiation* your sins has been forgiven once you receive salvation. *"without the shedding of blood there is no remission of sins. Because Christ has shed his blood for you; you are now free from the consequences of sins"-Hebrews 9:22*

But let me make this clear, if you do sin-you still have to go through the *process* of *repentance* by asking *God* to *forgive you & to cleanse you* of your sins. Then you have to make the effort by turning away from you're sins. You have to make a *180 degree* change from *wrong to right*. Which is known as *"metanoia" aka repentance? By having a change of mind & behavior in doing what's right in God's sight.*

The benefit of *propitiation*-it gives you the right to ask for forgiveness because of *Jesus Christ* sacrificial offering. **"Whom God set forth as a propitiation by His blood, through faith, to demonstrate His righteousness, because in His forbearance God had passed over the sins that were previously committed". (KJV) Romans 3:25**

Even in the *Old Testament propitiation* was initiated when the *High Priest* went into the *Tabernacle* to make atonement for his sins; as well as the sins of the *people of Israel*. **(KJV) Leviticus 4:35-"He shall remove all its fat, as the fat of the lamb is removed from the sacrifice of the peace offering. Then the priest shall burn it on the altar, according to the offerings made by fire to the Lord. So the priest shall make atonement for his sin that he has committed, and it shall be forgiven him".**

Propitiation was a sacrificial system that was always there in the beginning of the priesthood in the *Old Testament*. But in the *New Testament Jesus Christ* solidified it *once and for all*. "*We* observed that *Jesus* died for our sake & in our behalf. *Christ* took our place as a substitution for our sins, so that we may be *set free* from the *penalty of sin*".

John the Baptist claimed "*behold the lamb of God who takes away the sins of the world*".

The *Apostle Paul stated*-"*For He made Him who knew no sin to be sin for us, that we might become the righteousness of God in Him*".

Justification- In the *Greek l*anguage is the word "*dikaisos*" which denotes the act of *pronouncing righteousness*. It's where *God* makes you to be right with him. *H*e declares you to be righteous because of *Christ our Lord*. Because of the sacrifice he made for you on the *cross at Calvary*.

*T*he *bible* says that our righteousness is just as filthy rags, so it's the Lord that makes us to be righteous, not we ourselves. *Justification* also means to *justify*; which also indicates "*Just as I have not sinned*".

It is the *LORD* declaring sinners to be righteous in his sight, regardless of their sinful nature. *Apostle Paul* wrote, "*There is therefore now no condemnation to them which are in Christ Jesus, who walk not after the flesh, but after the Spirit*". *(KJV) Romans 8:1* Because of being *justified* you now live in Christ's strength & identity. "*The Lord's grace is enough for you & it gives you strength when you feel weak*". His favor gives you vitality to make it through so you can live out a *godly life*. *Jesus* becomes our *hope of glory* because he has made us to be right with the *almighty God*.

Reconciliation-in the *Greek language* is the word "*katallasso*"which means to exchange from being an enemy to becoming a friend. Once a person receives *redemption God* allows that individual who was formerly his enemy to be reconciled to him into a *friendly relationship*. *The LORD* ends up changing his attitude towards the sinner to be his friend instead of his enemy.

The death of *Christ* also brings to an end the enmity and estrangement which exist between *God & humankind*. Our hostility towards the LORD is removed because of *reconciliation* that came from *Jesus Christ*. *"And not only that, but we also rejoice in God through our Lord Jesus Christ, through whom we have now received the reconciliation".*

Jesus is the only person that can give you peace between you & the *almighty Father God. Christ* is the *"Prince of peace"*, who brings *reconciliation* to humankind through *redemption*. And once you become born again being reconciled to the *Father. "As his Children"*-you will also become *"Ministers of reconciliation"*, so you can help another to also be reconciled back to him. *2 Corinthians 5:17-18*

Glorification; is the last step in the process of *redemption* of the believer. And it begins on earth and it finds completion at *Christ returns*. In *Paul's* words **"Moreover whom he did predestinate, them he also called: and whom he called, them he also justified: and whom he justified, them he also glorified." (KJV) Romans 8:30**

Glorification is *multi-dimensional;* it involves the perfecting of the *spiritual nature* of the individual believer which takes place at death. When a believer passes into the presence of the *LORD?* It also involves the perfecting of the body of the believer, which will occur at the time of the resurrection in connection with the *second coming of Christ.* Which is a transformation of the entire body of the believer; by making you to be made *whole or holy?* For it is the completion of *redemption* when *God* exalts us after we die & go to *heaven*.

> ➢ *These spiritual benefits are so essential in the life of a believer. It is important to know that you are entitled to these benefits. And without redemption, you would not be able to acquire them. Redemption will free you from the guilt of your past mistakes. And it will give you hope for a better future.*
>
> When you are *redeemed*, it is *to be forgiven & to be made holy.* Redemption is the *back bone & the base* of a believer's *faith.*

Without *redemption* it would be impossible to live out your *faith walk with God.*

➤ *Yeah I know there are so many different religions*, but guess what, none of them offer *redemption. Redemption* only comes through *Jesus Christ* because he is the only person that died so you can have *eternal life. On that note:*

• If you do not know the *Lord Jesus Christ* in the pardon of your sins-*Today* is the day of your *salvation. "For God so loved the world that he gave his only begotten Son, Jesus Christ. Whoever believes in him will not perish but will have eternal life"*. The *Almighty God* wants you to have a relationship with him through *Jesus Christ.*

• If you would like to be <u>*saved*</u> & receive the wonderful *gift of <u>redemption, which also means salvation.</u>*

➤ <u>*Just Repeat this simple prayer;*</u> *say-Lord Jesus Christ, forgive me of my sins, help me to repent of my sins, cleanse me of my sins,*

• <u>*Come into my heart*</u>, *& into my life. I believe you are the Son of GOD, & you died for my sins, so I can have a relationship with you & eternal life. I receive & accept you, as my Savior, & also as my Lord. In Jesus Christ, name, (I pray amen).*

➤ <u>*After you recite this simple & effective prayer*</u>, *I believe this is your introduction to redemption. The Holy bible say's "with the heart, man believeth unto righteousness & with the mouth confession is made unto salvation". <u>(KJV) Romans 10:10</u>*

As an individual you have to proclaim & confess your salvation, so you can be saved. The Bible also states that "if you called on the name of Jesus Christ you will be saved. <u>(KJV) Romans 10:13</u>

➤ <u>*Then the next step*</u> *is to find a good bible base church in your neighborhood or in your City & start to Attend.*

To be *saved* also *exemplifies* that you will have a *relationship & eternal life* with *God* through his *son* the *Lord Jesus Christ.*

Salvation means to be *saved,* or to be *redeemed.* When you are *saved* it basically expresses that you become *born again*, which is a *spiritual new birth in Christ?-Read the Gospel of John 3:1-7 in the Holy Bible:*

* ❖ *Jesus Christ* is the *bridge* that will get you to the *Almighty God* & he is the *ladder* that will get you into heaven. *John 14:6*

Selah:14

THE GRACE & MERCY SUPPLIER

Metaphorically speaking; *Grace and mercy* are cousins, but *love* is the big brother. *Grace, mercy* & *love* are *related* and they all coincide with one another. You cannot have one without the other. *God* demonstrated his love towards you & I, while yet we were sinners. *(Romans 5:8) (NKJV)*

And because of this love; *grace* & *mercy* was birth. The *concept* of *God's mercy* deals with *God's forgiveness* towards an offender. *Mercy* is not getting what you do deserve. *Mercy is compassion* or *forgiveness* shown toward someone who cannot defend themselves. *And Grace is getting what you can't afford. Grace is the free and unmerited favor of God.*

God's mercy & *grace* is seen throughout the *scriptures.* Whether in the *Old* & *New Testament writings* within the *Holy bible?* Through *Christ* we are able to receive *God's grace* & *mercy.* The LORD has always demonstrated his *mercy and grace* to his children. No other person was able to do that except *Jesus. Christ* made it possible for *God's grace* & *mercy* to be shown & given.

Through the *salvation of the Lord, mercy and grace* was *established. "But God who is rich in mercy, for his great love wherewith he loved us" Ephesians 2:4 (KJV)*

"For by grace are ye saved through faith; and that not of yourselves: it is the gift of God" Ephesians 2:8 (KJV) You did nothing to deserve it but it is freely given from God. So for that reason, we need the *mercy & grace* of God. The *LORD* understands the weakness of our infirmities, which is the reason why? He has supplied us with his *grace & mercy.*

God knows you need his *mercy & grace* in order for you to get it right. For without his *grace and mercy* it would be impossible to live out your human existence on the *earth. As* a believer two of the perks that comes with being *saved, are the mercy & grace of God.* When you have the *grace of God* operating in your life it will cause wonderful things to happen for you. *Grace* will open doors that nobody can shut, & it will provide you with *opportunities.*

Now-when it comes to the *LORD's mercy* it will help you to get it right. *Especially* when you stumble or even fell in sin? It will uplift you & get you back on track.

As an example: when *Peter* denied the *Lord*, it was *God's mercy* that *forgave* and *restored him. As* far as the *Lord's grace* operating in *Peter's life*, it caused him to proclaim the *gospel in the book of Acts. And* he end up becoming a *great apostle,* who had an effective ministry.

God's Grace & mercy will work on your behalf because it demonstrates *his compassion, forgiveness & his goodness.* "**So then it is not of him who wills, nor of him who runs, but of God who shows mercy. "Thou in thy mercy hast led forth the people which thou hast redeemed: thou hast guided them in thy strength unto thy holy habitation". You in your mercy have led forth, The people whom You have redeemed; You have guided them in Your strength, To Your holy habitation. Exodus 15:13 (KJV)**

> ➤ ***God's Grace Through Christ:***

Grace *empowers your Salvation.* ***Grace*** *empowers Christ Living.* ***Grace*** *empowers you to be Generous Givers.* ***Grace*** *empowers you to serve God.* ***Grace*** *empowers Christian Ministry.* ***Grace*** *empowers those who are weak.* ***Grace*** *empowers your Relationship with God.* ***Grace*** *empowers you in times of need; &* ***Grace*** *empowers you to express Love to others.*

Selah:15

THE LIGHT BEARER

> ➤ *Then God said, "Let there be light"; and there was light.*<u>*Genesis1:3 (KJV)*</u>

<u>Definition</u>: <u>Light</u> *is spiritual enlightment that causes right living & it enables good deeds & it maintains hopeful views.*

<u>Synonym</u>: <u>Bearer</u>-*messenger, agent, conveyor, carrier, emissary*

Truly the light is sweet, and a pleasant thing it is for the eyes to behold the sun <u>*(KJV) Ecclesiastes 11:7*</u>

<u>*(KJV) John 1:7-*</u>*This man came for a witness, to bear witness of the Light, that all through him might believe.*

<u>*(KJV) John 8:12-*</u>*Then Jesus spoke to them again, saying, "I am the light of the world. He who follows Me will not walk in darkness, but will have the light of life."*

Light is illumination, it is the opposite of darkness. It deals with *spiritual enlightment & awareness*. The *bible* speaks of *light* as the *symbol* of *God's presence & his righteous activities*. <u>*1 John 1:5*</u>, states that *God is light and in him there is no darkness*. Matter of fact the *acronym* for **"<u>G</u>.<u>O</u>.<u>D</u>" is "<u>Greatness</u> <u>Over</u> <u>Darkness</u>"**.

Throughout the *Old Testament & New Testament* light is regularly associated with *God, his word, his salvation, his goodness, his truth & life.* The *scriptures* resonate with these themes, so that the *holiness of God* is presented in such a way. For *light* is *spiritual* but it is displayed in the *natural.*

Christ the *light* of the world exemplifies *God's attributes,* such as his *goodness, positivity* and *righteousness.* The *Lord* is also known as the *"Sun of righteousness", meaning* the *Son that brings the light of righteousness- Malachi 4:2 (KJV)*

Jesus illustrated, that he is the *light* of the world, whoever follows him will not walk in darkness but will have the *light of life. God* is also known as the *"Father of lights". "And every good and perfect gift is from above, & it comes down from him".* He does not change like shifting shadows. He is consistent in his *moral attributes* because *he is the same, yesterday, today & forevermore.*

For *God's light* represents *love, holiness and his righteousness.* I can't express that enough because that's who he is. It represents *his nature,* and if we are his children than we should also *exemplify these characteristics as well.* The bible says, *"He who practices righteousness is of God". 1 John 2:29 (KJV)* To practice something is to make an effort by doing it. It is a *process* that enables *improvement.*

The *LORD is a lamp unto your feet & the light unto your path.* Just like the *pillar of cloud* by *day, & the pillar of fire by night* leading his people (*Israel*). There for it is necessary to understand that there is no darkness in *God* because he is *Light.* He is the *torch of life* that shines in the *hearts of humanity.*

Imagine if *God's* light was absent in the *world,* there would be straight chaos. It is because of his light that the world is still rotating on its *axis.* Despite of the ignorance that takes place in *our society at times; God's presence helps to make the difference.*

And He does it through his marvelous light. For *God's light* will enable you to *act right. God's children* were created in his *image & likeness. In other words,* you were created to demonstrate his *characteristics*; as well as to function like him through *creativity.* That's what the *image & likeness* of *GOD* signifies.

For an *image* is a *reflection* of its *representation*. When you look in the mirror what do you see, is your *image*; which is you're *reflection*. But the image that I am talking about is the *image of Christ*. You were *predestined* to be *conformed* into his image.

Before the foundation of the world, *God* already had it in his mind that he wanted his *children* to be molded into the presentation of *Jesus Christ*.

As an example, if *GOD* is love, & you are *his child*. You should also *exemplify* love. How can you say you *love God* whom you have not seen, but hate your brother or sister that you do see? When you demonstrate *love towards* others then you are walking in the *light*. **Jesus said; "By this shall all men know that ye are my disciples, if ye have love one to another". John 13:35 (KJV)**

As a child of God; by your love for others & walking in integrity. It ensures that you belong to him. For *you* are a replica of your *Heavenly Father*. And he is counting on you to represent him through *his light. Jesus stated; "you are the light of the world, a city set on a hill that cannot be hidden. Y*ou were created to let your light shine. When you let it *shine*; in actuality you are making the *LORD* look *good. That's* what the scripture of *Matthew 5:16* is conveying, when you *"Let you're Light so shine; before men that they may see your good works & glorify your Heavenly father who is in heaven" (KJV)*

The light that it's referring to-is *spiritual truth* that pertains to *spiritual awareness* of *right living. And also by doing good deeds & making a difference. To let your light shine; it has to be through your actions by the way you carry yourself & live.* And that can only be done *by walking in the light & not in darkness.* For the opposite of light is darkness. Anything that is in darkness deals with *negativity, despair* and *wickedness.*

Which is the reason why the bible tells us, "that evil or bad company corrupts good habits"? Darkness corrupts & Light uplifts. So make the effort to stay away from darkness. *And walk in the light.*

As God's creation, when you let your light shine, you're allowing God's nature to work through you. "It is in him that you live, move & have your existence". The Apostle Paul said, "You are a living letter being read by others".

Sad to say, in this *millennium age* that we live in; some people are not concerned about their *integrity & dignity*. For some people the meaning of *good, means bad & the meaning of bad means good*. And those who are in the *light,* are acting like they are in the *dark*, & those who are in the *dark,* are behaving like they are in the *light*. *Just Confusion!!!*

It's even to the point, where some of these youngsters have no respect for those who are older than them. And some of these adults are not modeling on how the children should live. The children are the future and without the proper guidance that starts at home then they will go astray. For the LORD is a *God* of generations and he expresses himself through them. That's why we got "to *train up a child in the way they should live; so when they get old they won't be misguided"*. Proper social education for the children starts at *home*, & it carries out in the *schools. And it's enhance through our churches.*

The *Church* of the *Lord Jesus Christ* should be a *beacon of light* that influences the world; it should not be the other way around. *As a born again believer* it is your duty to set the example when it comes to shining *God's light. Jesus says*, **"I am the light of the world: he that followeth me shall not walk in darkness, but shall have the light of life. John 8:12 (KJV)**

The Lord also stated that a person does not light a candle & put it under a bushel. So why hide your light, or let it diminish. Your light is supposed to be seen & visible. *As Child of GOD;* you are suppose to be a *glory carrier*, & it is your duty for you to let your light shine. I know that we are not *perfect* but through *God's grace* we are able to let it shine.

> *The LORD is your everlasting Light (Isaiah 60:20) (KJV)*

The *LORD's light* is here to guide you so you can demonstrate *goodness. God's* light will keep you safe if you abide in it. Darkness always leads to *suffering and destruction.*

God loves you so much that he gave you knowledge, wisdom & understanding through his word the *Holy Bible. So you can walk in his marvelous light. God's word is a lamp unto your feet and a light unto your path that will guide* you in the right direction. The *word of God* provides you with *information & instructions that will bless & enhance your life.* You just got to put it into practice so you can see the results.

God's light is effective and it influences for the better. The *light signifies* "Good deeds", "Right *living*" & "Positive thinking", which is the *acronym* for "G.R.P". Once again remember your *light* is supposed to be *visible* so people can see it. *Especially,* when you live by the golden rule of life, which is; *"Doing unto others, as you want them to do unto you"; which also displays walking in the light.*

If you need assistance to walk in the light, the *LORD* will help you. He is always willing & able to give you the guidance that you need. It's all about the choices that you make that will determine your outcome. Its either you choose the *light or darkness.*

Love is also the substance of *light* because it *unites,* brings *peace* & it gives you *joy.* If you are walking in love, then you are also demonstrating the light of *God*; for *God* is love. Love is the most powerful vehicle in the universe because it reflects light. And that light will have a positive effect when it's *projected.* But you can only receive the light when you are connected to the *Source*; who is the *Almighty God & the Lord Jesus Christ.* *"For You will light my candle, The* LORD *my God will enlighten my darkness."* (KJV) <u>Psalm 18:28</u>

Because of sin the human nature needs the *light;* which is *Christ.* He is the only one that can *redeem you.* Even when you make mistakes he can get you back on track. The *LORD* is the remedy for darkness because he is the light. **"Arise, shine; for thy light is come, and the glory of the** LORD **is risen upon thee."-Isaiah 60:1 (KJV)**

Light always involves the removal of darkness in the *unfolding of biblical history and theology.* The contrast of light and darkness is common to all both in the *Old and New Testament.* The *Holy Bible* displays that *God* is *absolute sovereign,* who rules over the powers of darkness. The *Lord Jesus Christ gained the victory & overcame darkness at the Cross at Calvary. "It is finished, that's what he said"-***Believe in the light while you have the light, so that you may become children of light". <u>John 12:36 (KJV)</u>**

Selah:16

THE CARPENTER

Definition: **Carpenter** *is a builder and a repairer of broken things.*

Synonym: *builder, inventor, creator, maker, manufacturer, craftsperson,*

(KJV) Isaiah 44:13-The carpenter stretcheth out his rule; he marketh it out with a line; he fitteth it with planes, and he marketh it out with the compass, and maketh it after the figure of a man, according to the beauty of a man; that it may remain in the house.

(KJV) Matthew 16:18-And I also say to you that you are Peter, and on this rock I will build My church, and the gates of Hades shall not prevail against it.

(KJV) Mark 6:3-Is this not the carpenter, the Son of Mary, and brother of James, Joses, Judas, and Simon? And are not His sisters here with us?" So they were offended at Him.

When it comes to drawing up a blue print & building from it, the *Almighty God* is the *Architect*. He knows how to place each & every piece together to complete the puzzle. He specializes in *configuration* that leads to *construction*.

Before the *LORD* builds anything, he first thinks & then draws out the *specs*. He is the *"ELOHIM"* the *Supreme Creator* of the entire *Universe*. When the *Almighty God* created the *Heavens & the Earth* in the book of *Genesis,* he did it one time. *God* is very smart; whatever he *created,* he planted the *seed* within it, so it can re-produce itself.

Every male being or creature have seeds within themselves, so they can *procreate* after *its* own kind. *God* set up this creative *system,* so he wouldn't have to step off his *throne from heaven to re-create again.* That's what a *master builder* does is set up a firm foundation that will last from *Generation* to generations.

It took *God six days* to *create* what he had in his mind & on the *seventh day* he rested from all his work. What you need to understand is when *God* rested that doesn't mean that he was tired. The *LORD* can never be tired because he is *eternal.* But he was resting from what he already created in his mind. In other words the blue print for his will for the *Earth & Humanity.*

> ➤ *Expression of God's Creative Power-Genesis chapter 1 & 2*

God created light & he separated it from darkness-1ˢᵗ day of Creation,

God separate the sky from water on the earth-2ⁿᵈ day of Creation,

God separated the land from the water. Then he created plants-3ʳᵈ day of Creation,

God created the sun, moon & stars-4ᵗʰ day of Creation,

God created the fish to fill the ocean & the birds for the sky-5ᵗʰ day of Creation,

God created animals & human beings-6ᵗʰ day of Creation,

7ᵗʰ day, God ended his work which he had made; and he rested on from all his work. Then God blessed the seventh day and sanctified it. After God saw his creative work, he said it was very Good.

The *almighty God* created planet earth with *specifics, formats & arrangements.* He placed & set things in order so he wouldn't have to *reconstruct again.*

He created the earth to *reproduce* after its own kind. Once he displays his creative works then the *LORD* builds purposes for what he *created*. *God* knows the *end* from the *beginning* and he also knows the *middle*. *He is the Alpha & the Omega.*

Look at what he said to Jeremiah, "*before you were even formed & born I knew you & I ordained you & sanctified you to be a prophet*". *God* already had *Jeremiah* in his mind, way before the foundation of the earth. And at the appointed time, he willed *Jeremiah* into *being*. It's the same thing for you, *God* had you in his mind & then he willed for you to *exist*. The *LORD* created the earth to accomplish his will for his *good pleasure* & he added you into his *equation*.

You and I come from his *divine manuscript* that he built in his mind. Which is the reason why; life is like a movie & everyone are here to play a role? Therefore you cannot put the *Almighty God* in a box because he is not just a *religious God;* he is a *Creator of all*.

1 Corinthians 3:9 (KJV), says that "*we are co-workers with God, you are God's field & you are his building*". *The LORD creates through humanity to accomplish his will on planet earth. In order for God to build* on the earth, he needs individuals to do so. The *LORD* works through people, he needs *human beings* so his purpose can be *fulfilled*.

Footnote-*It is always a privilege to be used by the Almighty God; especially when he's creating through you*-"*Never be prideful when God uses you, always be humble & grateful*".

Of course, God will bless you & reward you. But the focus is about his accomplishments. When *Jesus Christ* was on earth, especially during the time of his *private ministry?* His *teachings* were based on the *Gospel of the Kingdom. His focused was to train & prepare his disciples to carry out his work after his departure.*

Jesus Christ was known as the *carpenter's son* because *of his father's trade*. In the *Jewish* culture whatever *occupation the father* acquired; was usually passed down to the *male child*. It was stated that the father of his household would train his son at the age of twelve in whatever field of occupation he was involved in. (*Mark 6:3)(KJV)*

*T*heologians and Biblical scholars suggest that *Christ* was also a *carpenter* because of his *father Joseph?* His earthly father *Joseph* was skilled in carpentry. The *Greek word* for *carpenter* is *"tekton"*, which means *builder*. A *carpenter* is a person who builds things with *his hands. But Jesus Christ* was a builder of *people.*

Jesus said to Peter, "upon this rock I will build my church & the gates of hell will not prevail against it". The *Lord* understood that his building was not based on a *facility*, but it was based on *peoples*. That's why his *church* is known as the *body of Christ. He is the head and we are his body.* The *Lord's carpentry work* was to establish *God's heavenly kingdom on the earth through his followers.*

The *body of Christ* is the *Lord's <u>heart</u>, <u>hands</u>, <u>feet</u> & his <u>mouth piece</u>. And* it's through you that the *Lord* accomplishes his *work.* Whether it's by having you to spread the *Gospel?* Or by having you to set up *godly networks on earth such; as <u>Ministries</u>, <u>Businesses</u>, <u>Hospitals</u>, <u>Schools</u> & etc.*

<u>*True leader's* creates other *leaders*</u>. Great leaders are not intimidated by other potential leaders. I think one of the problems that we face in our society is the lack of *mentorship.* <u>Whether it be</u>-in our *churches*, or in the *activism* arena, or just in our *work place.*

Some *leaders are insecure & self-fish*. They keep their *information & mentoring* to themselves, instead of passing it on to *others*. It's about depositing unto others so the world can continue to evolve. <u>*Stats*</u> say's, a leader who does not have a successor, *fails as a leader*. It's not about you, but it's about the future *generation* to come; so God's purpose can be fulfilled on the earth.

The LORD is a *God of generation*. And he is not only concerned about the now, but also about the future. Which is the reason why *Jesus Christ* poured into his disciples, so they can pour into others? Because of *Jesus* discipleship; now the *body of Christ* is worldwide. *Discipleship is the reproduction of others and it comes through building.*

God is looking for *spiritual carpenters* who are willing to *build* his Kingdom & people. <u>That's what *carpenters* do</u>-is <u>*train,*</u> <u>*inspire,*</u> <u>*edify,*</u> <u>*uplift*</u> & <u>*build.*</u> The *Lord* is a *master builder,* but he also needs other builders to carry out his work. Every *builder* needs assistants that will *undergird & uphold* their hands, so they can get the job done. Just like <u>*Moses,*</u> <u>*Joshua,*</u> <u>*Nehemiah*</u> & countless of others in the bible.

JEHOVAH-JIREH will provide you with the necessary tools that you need to get the job done. Whether it's *people, finances, property, anointing, gifting, ability, intelligence, wisdom, knowledge & understanding? Just whatever you need to accomplish the task,* <u>*Don't worry*</u>*-He shall supply.*

Jesus is not only the *carpenter's son,* but he is the carpenter himself. That will give you the blueprint in order for you to build. Just like how he had *Noah* build the <u>*Ark,*</u> & *Moses* build the <u>*Tabernacle*</u>; & *King Solomon* to build the <u>*Temple.*</u>

God is a *kingdom* & *people* builder. *He is concerned about your character, and the way you treat others.* He understands that your *gift* will get you *in*; but it's your *character* that will *keep you.* The *"Sermon on the Mount"* teachings were *kingdom principles* designed to build his followers *spiritually & morally? Seeing the crowds, he went up on the mountain, and when he sat down, his disciples came to him.*

The *LORD* wants to build his *people* so they can be *whole in their lives. God* is a *builder* of *people* & not just *property.* The work of a carpenter is to *inspire, motivate, encourage, inform & to edify.* The *Almighty God* builds us up, so we can eventually build others for his *purpose & glory. Thy Kingdom come; thy will be done on Earth, just as it is in Heaven. Selah!!!*

*T*HE HOLY *S*PIRIT *A*KA *T*HE *H*OLY *G*HOST

Selah: 17

THE COMFORTER

(KJV) John 14:16-And I will pray the Father, and he shall give you another Comforter, that he may abide with you forever;

(KJV) John 14:26-But the Comforter, which is the Holy Ghost, whom the Father will send in my name, he shall teach you all things, and bring all things to your remembrance, whatsoever I have said unto you.

A comforter is a person or thing that provides *consolation*. It also guides and sustains. The *comforter* that I am speaking of is the almighty *God*, operating as the *third person* in the *Holy Trinity*. *The third person is* known as the "*Holy Spirit*" or the "*Holy Ghost*".

The *Holy Spirit* is known in the *Greek language* as the *"paracletos"*, which is translated as an "*Advocate*" or "*Helper*", meaning one who comes along side. *Paraclete* comes from the "*koine*" *Greek* word which signifies "one who consoles or comforts". It also intercedes on your behalf, as an advocate in court. The word for *paraclete* is passive in form, *etymologically*. The *Holy Spirit* operates as *God's active* force and *intercessor*.

It was always there in the beginning as a mediator when *God* was creating the *Heavens & the Earth*. "*Genesis 1:2*" states that "the *spirit* moved upon the face of the waters. And then *God* said let there be *light: and there was light*". *(KJV)*

The *Holy Ghost* is *God's assisting tool. God* speaks it, & *then the Holy Spirit* makes it happen. *God* is the painter & the *Holy Spirit* is the paint brush that assists in the *LORD's creativity.* The *Holy Spirit* is *God's* agent that works for him. *The Almighty God* usually works through the *Holy Spirit* to do his work on the *Earth.* The *Holy Spirit* comes along side *the Son* to accomplish *God's will. Our Heavenly Father God the Creator* is "*3 in one*", & *He is "1 in three".* In other words, *God* can act independent of himself & he can also work together, as *3 persons-The Holy Trinity.*

When *God* created the *Heavens & the Earth,* he *acted* as the (*Creator & Father*). And when he needed to *redeem humanity* he sent himself, as the (*Son Jesus Christ the Savior*). And when he needed to *birth the Church,* he sent himself as the (*Mighty rushing wind aka the Holy Ghost*). "*That's how Great & Almighty God* is"

God is able to do whatever he pleases. He is the *Triune God,* who is *all sufficient within himself.* The *Holy Ghost* has many *descriptions & functions.* He is a *comforter,* an *advocator,* a *teacher,* a *guide,* a *counselor* & also an *active force.*

*Footnote-*The *Holy Spirit* was given so you can *have power to do God's will* on this earth. It was not only just given, so you can run around the church & do the *holy ghost shuffle & cartwheels.*

The *Holy Spirit* was given to the believers to be effective on the *earth. God's spirit* lives *within born again believers.* Having the *Holy Spirit* gives you proof that you *belong to God, the Father & to the Lord Jesus Christ. Because the spirit itself bears witness with our spirit that we are children of the Most high God. And, "If children, then heirs with God, & joint-heirs with Christ". Romans 8:14-17, states that, those who are led by the spirit of God are his children. "For you were not given a spirit of bondage to fear but you receive the spirit of adoption, whereby you cry Abba, Father.*

The true meaning of having the *Holy Ghost* it's not just because you speak in tongues, even though that's one of the evidence. But the most important evidence is the power that you demonstrate to do the *LORD's* Will. Expressing *love towards* others, also displays love as being the main *evidence. **Jesus, says by this people will know that you are my disciples, if you have love for one another.** **John 11:35 (KJV)***

Matter of fact; one of the main *fruits of the spirit* is Love. "*Whoever claims to love God yet hates a brother or sister is a liar.* Operating in love within the *body of Christ* is one of the signs that displays that you have the *holy spirit*. For *God is Love, and if you are his child & you have his DNA, you should also exemplify love to others.*

God sent the Holy Spirit to guide & to comfort his children after the ascension of *Jesus Christ*. The *Holy Spirit* also distributed *gifts to the church*, such as, "*spiritual & ministry*" Gifts. It also provided *spiritual fruits* to edify the *body of Christ*.

The *Holy Ghost* is a *gentleman*, it does not force himself on you. You have to want it, in order to receive it. But it is available to you through *Christ*. For *it is a must to have the Holy Spirit*. You cannot live out a *godly life* without the *Holy Ghost*. It will convict you when you are *wrong*, & it will comfort you when you need *upliftment*.

*R*emember the *Holy Spirit* is *God's active force* working in the life of a *believer*. That's why the *Lord* had to go away so you can receive the *Holy Spirit*. Because *Jesus* knew that you would need it.

In the *Old Testament* the *Holy Spirit* was upon *God's chosen people* "*Israel*". It led them by a *pillar of fire by night & by a pillar of cloud by day*. *B*ut in the *New Testament* the Holy Ghost resides within a *born again believer*. Your body becomes the temple of the *Holy Spirit once you become born again & receive its baptism.*

In the "*Gospel of Luke chapter 11 verse 9 &10 & 13*"-*Jesus* says, "*So I say to you: Ask and it will be given to you; seek and you will find; knock and the door will be opened to you.*

For everyone who *Asks-receives*; the one who *Seeks-finds*; and to the one who *Knocks-the door will be open*. *How much more will your Father in heaven give the Holy Spirit to those who ask him? Also* when-"**you repent and be**

baptized in the name of Jesus Christ, you will receive the gift of the Holy Spirit". _Acts 2:38 (KJV)_

> _Spiritual & Ministry Gifts of the Holy Spirit._

Romans 12:6-8 Motivational Gift of a Perceiver Motivational Gift of a Server Motivational Gift of a Teacher Motivational Gift of an Exhorter Motivational Gift of a Giver Motivational Gift of an Administrator Motivational Gift of Compassion

1 Corinthians 12:7-10 Manifestation Gift of Word of Wisdom Manifestation Gift of Word of Knowledge Manifestation Gift of Faith Manifestation Gift of Healing Manifestation Gift of Working of Miracles Manifestation Gift of Prophecy Manifestation Gift of Discerning of Spirits Manifestation Gift of Various kinds of Tongues Manifestation Gift of Interpretation of Tongues

Ephesians 4:11-13

> _Ministry gifts of the Church (the body of Christ)_

Ministry Gift of Apostle Ministry Gift of Prophet Ministry Gift of Evangelist Ministry Gift of Pastor Ministry Gift of Teacher

> THE FRUIT OF THE _HOLY SPIRIT (GALATIANS 5:22-23)_

LOVE-John 15:12-14

JOY- 1 Peter 1:8

PEACE-Philippians 4:7

PATIENCE-1Thessalonians 5:14

KINDNESS-Proverbs 11:16

GOODNESS-Titus 3:8

FAITHFULNESS-Psalm 89:5

GENTLENESS-1 Peter 3:15

SELF-CONTROL -Titus 2:12

JEHOVAH SHALOM aka
PRINCE OF PEACE

Selah:18

THE PEACE MAKER

Jehovah Shalom the *GOD* of peace, or prosperity. *Jehovah* had appeared to him, and saluted him by saying *"Peace be unto thee*,"- *"Then Gideon built an altar there unto the* Lord, *and called it Jehovah shalom: unto this day it is yet in Ophrah of the Abiezrites." **Judges 6:24 (KJV)***

For unto us a child is born, unto us a son is given, and the government shall be upon his shoulders. And he will be called Wonderful Counselor, *Mighty God*, Everlasting Father, Prince of Peace. ***Isaiah 9:6 (KJV)***

Peace is a state of assurance. It is the lack of fear & a sense of tranquility. It is *fellowship, harmony, & unity* between individuals. *Peace* is freedom from worry, disturbance & oppression thoughts. *God* has reconciled humanity through the peace of *Christ*.

The *Almighty God* desires his children to live in peace & to have tranquility of mind. *God* doesn't want you to live in distress being stress out. So many people are stress because of the life issues they deal with. Life can be challenging at times and it can knock you off your balance. But you got to know that *God* wants you to *"cast your worries upon him because he cares for you"*.

The *LORD* is *strong & mighty* who is able to handle your life issues. Whenever you feel cornered and your back is up against the wall; call on the name of *Jesus Christ*. And watch him deliver you & give you *peace*. *The* *Almighty God* provides peace through his *Son Jesus Christ*.

Remember the *Lord* is a peace maker & he is able to give you peace in the midst of your storms. Matter of fact; he will rise up & say *peace be still*, so you can have *rest*. The *acronym* for "**R.E.S.T**" is "**Release Every Struggle** **Totally**". When you release your struggle & give it to *God*. Then he will exchange it, & give you peace.

See the peace that the world offers you is different from the peace that *Christ* provides. The peace that the world provides deals with substances, such as *alcohol, drugs & illicit sex.* These types of substances are temporary because they only sedate you for a moment. True *peace comes* from knowing that *God loves & cares* about you. And that he would do whatever it takes to sustain you. ***Jesus said, peace I leave with you, my peace I give you.*** ***I do not give it to you as the world gives it. Do not let your heart be*** ***troubled & do not be afraid. John 14:27 (KJV)***

God wants you to rely on him in the midst of your troubles. He wants to be your shield of *faith* and *your peacemaker*. He wants to give you the *peace* *that surpasses all understanding.* The type of *peace of mind,* that will help you weather your storms.

Now; beside the *LORD* being your peacemaker, he also wants you to live a life of peace. ***"Blessed are the peacemakers: for they will be called*** ***the children of God. Matthew 5:9 (KJV)*** *This passage of scripture is* *illustrating that* a *child of God* will be *bless* when they exemplify *peace*. As God's children we should always try our best to *pursue peace* with others. Not saying it's going to be easy at times but you should make an effort to do so. *Peace* produces *harmony* that helps to maintain *relationships*. Without peace it would be quite hard to function & to get along with others. *Chaos & confusion* is the absence of *peace*. *God* is not the *author of* *confusion* because he is a *peacemaker*. And if you are his child he expects for *you to be the same. Selah!!!*

THE KINGDOM ESTABLISHER (KING OF KINGS)

- *For God is the King of all the earth; Sing praises with understanding.* **(KJV) Psalm 47:7**

The <u>Hebrew</u> word for *kingdom* is *"mamlakah"*-meaning to *reign or rule.*

The <u>Greek</u> word for *kingdom* is *"basileia"*- meaning *sovereignty or royal power.*

*A K*ingdom is a territory ruled over by a *King;* it refers to a *King's authority or dominion.*

Biblically speaking the *Kingdom of God* is the *universal* sphere that covers *the Heavens & the Earth.* It is a *spiritual realm* where the *Almighty God* rules and makes his decisions to *Govern.* The *Kingdom of God* rules over all intelligence in *heaven* and on *planet earth.*

God's Kingdom is the experience of *blessedness* like of the *Garden of Eden.* It represents <u>*power,*</u> <u>*authority,*</u> <u>*purpose,*</u> *& <u>effectiveness.</u>*

The *Garden of Eden* in the book of *Genesis* was considered to be *Adam's kingdom of heaven* because of his *authority to rule.* The *Kingdom of heaven* deals with rulership on *earth* through *Jesus Christ. Adam* was in charge of the garden as the *sole proprietor owner*. God gave *Adam* dominion to rule over the animals and to maintain *stewardship.*

The concept of God's kingdom is vast because it displays his decision making & also his delegation. The Almighty God establishes his kingdom through his board of directors, which is the Lord Jesus Christ & the Holy Spirit. He also establishes his kingdom on earth through his servants, "the body of Christ".

The Kingdom of God & Heaven are used interchangeably based on the context of the scriptures in the bible. The Kingdom of Heaven has been manifested in various aspects throughout the Bible & Centuries. In the theocratic aspect it was establish by <u>Moses, the Judges of Israel, King David, King Solomon & the Lord Jesus Christ</u>. And in this millennium dispensation it continues with <u>the Church, the body of Christ</u>.

The Church is a representation of the Holy Trinity on the earth; as the Father, the Son & the Holy Ghost. God has made the Church to be a platform, so he can establish his Kingdom. Believers of the Lord Jesus Christ are known as kingdom builders; as well as establishers. In God's original mandate in "<u>Genesis 1,v26-28</u>"-He wants his children to <u>replenish, subdue</u> & to have <u>dominion</u> on planet earth. For the kingdom of God is not in word, but in power. <u>1st Corinthians 4:12 (KJV)</u>

*Christ wants his body to exemplify his kingdom to the world; so the church can set the example. In biblical times, Jesus mighty works were intended to prove that the Kingdom of God had come upon his followers. His parables illustrated to His disciples the truth about the Kingdom of God. And when He taught His followers to pray, at the heart of their petition were the words, **"Thy kingdom come, thy will be done on earth as it is in heaven".** <u>Matthew 6:10 (KJV)</u>*

*On the eve of His death, He assured His disciples that He would yet share with them the happiness and the fellowship of the Kingdom (<u>Luke 22:22-30</u>). **"And He promised that He would appear again; on the earth in glory to bring the blessedness of the Kingdom, to those for whom it was prepared" <u>Matthew 25:31-34 (KJV)</u>***

The Holy bible gives us several indications when it comes to pertaining to the Kingdom of God & Heaven. Jesus made many references about the teaching of the Gospel of the Kingdom. Which deals with life principles based on the "Sermon on the Mount"? The presence and coming of the Kingdom of God was the central message of Jesus. For example, his teaching was designed to show men how they might enter the Kingdom of God.

In the Gospel of John ch 3; "Jesus spoke to Nicodemus & told him that he had to be "born again" in order to, "see the kingdom", & then he had to be "baptized" by water & the holy spirit to, "enter the kingdom". Which indicates that they are some prerequisite in order to become part of God's Kingdom.

The term *"Kingdom of God"* occurs *four times* in *Matthew 12:28; 19:24; 21:31; 21:43, fourteen times* in *Mark, thirty-two times* in *Luke,* twice in the *Gospel of John 3:3, 5, six times* in *Acts, eight times* in Paul, and *once* in *Revelation 12:10.*

The bible also states that the Kingdom of God is within you. *"And when he was demanded of the Pharisees, when the kingdom of God should come, he answered them and said, The kingdom of God cometh not with observation: Neither shall they say, Lo here! or, lo there! for, behold, the kingdom of God is within you." Luke 17:20-21 (KJV)*

In suggestion; if you are a *born again believer God* has placed his *kingdom purpose* within your *heart.* And in due season he will unravel it. That's why you have to be about your *father's business* & stay focus. *Kingdom business is serious business, and the LORD is looking for faithful stewards who will build to make an impact!!!*

Selah: 20

THE INNOVATOR

Definition: *An* **Innovator** is a person who introduces *new ideas*; & who is *creative* in *thinking*. They introduce *new ways & methods* of doing things.

Example-The *New Testament* was a new concept based of the *Old Testament*. The *Old Testament* is *interrelated* with the *New Testament* but they are different from one another. The *Old Testament* was based on the *"Law"* & the *New Testament* is based on *"Grace"*.

The bible states that God is the same *yesterday, today & forever*. He *sees* the past, *present, & future* all at the same time, because he is *eternal*. But when it comes to him acting on the earth, his eternal nature attributes to him being *progressive*. Everything the *LORD* did during the *biblical times* & in *world history* he always did it with progression in *mind*. *God* is not in the business of *staleness and stagnation*. He is an *innovative God* who always finds new ways to accomplish his will.

His principles remains the same but his methods do change. *God* is about forward *thinking and innovation*. Beside him being powerful; he is also *intelligent & progressive*. I believe in this millennium age that we are living in; the *LORD* is calling the body of *Christ* to be *creative & progressive*. Because doing the same thing over & over out of routine can cause *stagnation*. Whether it's dealing with your *worship services, or your yearly conferences?*

God wants the church to be *creative & relevant* in these times we are living in. But still maintain its *integrity & dignity.* The *LORD* wants you to be creative when it comes to proclaiming the *Gospel;* as well as uplifting his *Kingdom.*

Operating in tradition is good to some degree, but it can cause irrelevancy if there's no change. What we need to realize is anything that you do repetitively without change, you will eventually get tired of. It's good to do something's differently at times.

Even the miracles the *Lord Jesus Christ* performed in scriptures were always different. It was rarely that he performed the same miracles twice. My point is as a child of *God* it's good to be innovative; especially when it comes to doing *Ministry* & building *God's Kingdom. Let's* be fresh in our approach when it comes to doing ministry work in our churches; let's make it *exciting and innovative.*

The *LORD* wants to do something new but we got to be willing to flow with him. **"Remember not the former things, nor consider the things of old. Behold, I am doing a new thing; now it springs forth, do you not perceive it? I will make a way in the wilderness and rivers in the desert.** **Isaiah 43:18-19** **(KJV)**-The *Almighty God* is a *thinker,* He is *innovative.* The *LORD* does not want us to keep on doing the same things out of routine or tradition. He wants you & I to be innovative just like him. That's why he created us in his likeness to function like him when it comes to being *innovative. Selah!!!*

Selah: 21

THE AUTHOR & FINISHER

Looking unto *Jesus*, the *author* and *finisher* of our faith, who for the joy that was set before Him endured the cross, despising the shame, and has sat down at the right hand of the throne of *God*. **<u>Hebrews 12:2 (KJV)</u>**

*F*rom the book of "<u>Genesis</u> to <u>Revelation</u>", *Christ* is seen throughout the whole scriptures. He is seen from the seed of the woman up to his *ascension*. The *Lord Jesus Christ* was with the *father* from the beginning of *Creation*, & now he sits at the right hand of *God*.

"In the beginning God created the Heavens & the Earth". The earth was without form, and void; and darkness was on the face of the deep. And the Spirit of God was hovering over the face of the waters. Then God said, "Let there be light"; and there was light. <u>Genesis 1:1-3 (KJV)</u>

The Holy Trinity was all part of the creative process in the beginning in Genesis. "God as the Creator", "the Holy Spirit as the Active force"-moving upon the face of the waters & "the Lord Jesus Christ as the source of light".

Besides the natural light in the book of Genesis; Jesus was the spiritual light that God was referring too in "verse 3", when he said, "let there be light & then light became". God created this earth through Jesus Christ. "Because all things were made through him & without him was not anything made".

The light also refers to God being the base of our *existence, & Jesus Christ* as the *redeemer* of our *soul*. Which makes the *Father* & the *Son* to be the Author & *finisher of our faith? Everything* starts & ends with them. *"I am the Alpha and Omega, the beginning and the ending, saith the Lord which is, and which was, and which is to come, the Almighty".* <u>*Revelation 1:8 (KJV)*</u>

Alpha and Omega; is the *first & last letter* of the Greek *alphabet,* which is used in the *Holy Bible* to express the *eternity of God.* These letters became a *favorite symbol* of the *eternal divinity* of our *Lord.* Both *Greeks* & *Hebrews* employed the letters of the alphabet as numerals to exemplify the *LORD's infinite nature.*

- *Here is a list of the different biblical teachings based on the LORD being the <u>Author</u> & <u>finisher</u>.*

➤ **<u>Theology</u>**-is the study of *God's N*ature & *B*ible truth. It expresses the *LORD's attributes & his ways of getting things done.* Within theology you also have <u>*Systematic theology,*</u> *which addresses theological topics one by one (God, Sin, Humanity) & etc. And it attempts to summarize all the biblical teaching on each particular subject.*

➤ ***<u>Systematic Theology</u>*** deals with the different doctrines based on the *inspiration* of the *H*oly Scriptures. <u>such as,</u>

- *"<u>Bibliology</u>" is the study of the sacred writings of the Holy Bible.*

- *"<u>Anthropology</u>" is the study of Man or Human kind,*

- *"<u>Hamartiology</u>" is the study of sin*

- *"<u>Christology</u>" is the study of Jesus Christ,*

- *"<u>Soteriology</u>" is the study of Salvation.*

- *"<u>Ecclesiology</u>" is the study of the Church.*

- *"Pneumatology" is the study of the Holy Spirit.*

- *"Angeology" is the study of Angels.*

- *& "Eschatology" is the study of the last days or things to Come.*

➢ *Within each doctrine* the *Almighty God & the Lord Jesus Christ* plays a *vital role* within them. These fundamental teaching's captures the essence of the *human nature,* & also of the *Almighty God. F*or the *LORD* can only be *explained* to a limited degree but he is mostly *revealed* through *our conscience & experiences.*

➢ The explaining takes place from the *"Holy Scriptures"* and the revealing is expressed through our *"Life existence".*

The LORD is *mysterious*; as well as *personable.* And he enjoys fellowship with those who belongs to him. *As a*uthor & *f*inisher of your faith, everything starts & ends with, *"The Almighty & the Lord"*-when it comes to his *Creation.*

The *book* of *"Acts chapter seventeen verse 24-25"*, states that *"God* made the world and everything in it, since He is *Lord* of *Heaven & Earth,* does not dwell in temples made with hands. Nor is He worshiped with men's hands, as though He needed anything, since He gives to all life, breathe, and all things".*(KJV)*

All Scripture is given by inspiration of God, and is profitable for doctrine, for reproof, for correction, for instruction in righteousness, that the man of God may be complete, thoroughly equipped for every good work-2Timothy 3:16 (KJV)

So it's through the *Holy Bible* that the *LORD* is able to give you instructions for your betterment. Because you are his *Creation* & he wants the best for you. You were created in his *image, & in his likeness* to carry out his *attributes* on *planet earth.*

*T*he *LORD* is a prolific *a*uthor who writes out your life manual script based on his *purpose for you. "All things is working together for your good"* because he is the one who is *orchestrating it.*

*T*hat's what an *A*uthor does, is write out the <u>*Introduction*</u>; as well as the <u>*Body*</u> & the <u>*Conclusion*</u> to your *life story. So others can read it.* "We are *living epistles*", *read by many.* The *Church* is *Christ representatives,* & we are here to represent his *Kingdom.* We are Kingdom *citizens* of a *holy nation* made up of <u>*Prophets*</u>, <u>*Priests*</u> & <u>*Servants*</u>.

The *Almighty God* is the *Sovereign Ruler* of the *Heavens* & *the Earth.* He is the *KING* of all kings, & the *LORD* of all lords. He is the "*ELOHIM*", the *Supreme God* of all. He has total *Dominance and Authority.*

*T*he word *kingdom* is a compound word which is two words in one, <u>*"King"*</u> <u>*"Dominion"*</u>. The *Almighty God* is the absolute ruler over his *Kingdom.* No one *elected him,* & nobody can *impeach him.* He is the "<u>*Chairman*</u> & the <u>*CEO*</u>" over the "*Heavens*" and the entire "*Universe*".

*H*is *board of directors* is the "<u>*Lord Jesus Christ*</u> & <u>the *Holy Spirit*</u>". And his *staff members* are his "<u>*Angels*</u> & <u>*Archangels*</u>", who works out his *assignments.* His *pillar establishers* are his "<u>*Servants*</u>"-<u>the body of Christ</u> aka <u>the Church</u>, who carries out his will on the *earth.*

As author & *finisher, Jesus said to his disciples, I will give you the keys of the kingdom of heaven, whatever you bind on earth will be bound in heaven,* & *whatever you loose on earth, will be loosed in heaven.* The *keys Jesus referred to exemplify* <u>*"power"*</u> & <u>*"authority"*</u>. *Jesus Christ gave his servants the power* & *authority to accomplish their Kingdom assignment on the earth.*

The Gospel of *Matthew, Mark, Luke* & *John* was all based on the *Life of Christ*; as well as on the *Kingdom of God* & *Heaven.* That's why the teachings of *Christ* on earth were based on the "Gospel of the *K*ingdom". The *Sermon on the Mount* was teachings based on the principle expressions of the *kingdom.* The entire *Holy bible* from "*Genesis to Revelation*" is based on "*Salvation*", "*Life living principles*" & "*God's kingdom authority*".

The *Kingdom of God* & *Heaven* is built on *love, truth, effectiveness* & *light. God's Kingdom resides* within every believer and it's displayed by *power.* "*The kingdom suffers violence* & *the violence takes it by force*". *The force signifies God's authoritative power. And if you are a Kingdom builder for real; then act upon his might.*

The *Church* is part of the *Kingdom of God,* & it is a very important *element.* It is based on what he wants to accomplish through his *chosen vessels.* For it is in him that *we live, move & have our being. Jesus* sits at the right hand of *God* making intercession for his *church,* so he can give *his body* the victory to *overcome.*

For whatever is *born* of *God* overcomes the world & our *faith* gives us the *victory.* As *born again* believers we have access to our inheritance as *Kingdom Citizen's & Ambassador's.* The *a*uthor of our faith has accepted us and we are sitting in heavenly places because of him. The *Lord* made it possible to connect with him through his work on the *cross* & also *by* your *faith?*

The Lord is the Author & *f*inisher of our faith, who has declared that we win at the end because he has gone before us to give us the *victory.* **"For whatever is born of God overcomes the world & our faith gives us the victory". "But thanks be to God, which gives us victory through our Lord Jesus Christ".** <u>**1 Corinthians 15:57 (KJV)**</u>

GOD is the Product-the Almighty; who *blesses, inspires, edifies, motivates, encourages, provides, heals, protects & sustains those who belong to him.* The *LORD* is everything that you need because he is the *source of life.* He is the *"EL-Shaddai",* the *"All Sufficient One". H*e can do it all because he his *"Omnipotent", "Omnipresent" & "Omniscient'.*

*N*obody can exist outside of *God* because he is the very air that we breathe. He is the *Author & finisher, the alpha & omega* of our existence. *"Salute & Honor, and All Glory goes to Our Heavenly Father & to Our Lord & Savior!!!* <u>*Hallelujah!!!*</u>

THE *ALMIGHTY GOD*(ABBA) & *THE LORD JESUS CHRIST* IS THE *ULTIMATE GREATEST*!!! & THE *BEST FOREVER*!!!

- ➤ **Definition**: **Greatest**-*of ability, quality, or eminence considerably above the normal or average.*

  - • **Definition: Best**-*of the most excellent, effective, or desirable type or quality.*

- ➤ **"Great is our Lord, and of great power: his understanding is infinite."- Psalm 147:5 (KJV)**

Hast thou not known? hast thou not heard, that the everlasting God, the LORD, *the Creator of the ends of the earth, fainteth not, neither is weary? there is no searching of his understanding.* **KJV) Isaiah 40:28**

For the LORD *your God is God of gods, and Lord of lords, a great God, a mighty, and a terrible, which regardeth not persons, nor taketh reward:* **(KJV) Deuteronomy 10:17**

For as much as there is none like unto thee, O LORD; thou art great, and thy name is great in might. *(KJV)* **Jeremiah 10:6**

For the LORD is great, and greatly to be praised: he is to be feared above all gods. *(KJV)* **Psalm 96:4**

Thine, O LORD is the greatness, and the power, and the glory, and the victory, and the majesty: for all that is in the heaven and in the earth is thine; thine is the kingdom, O LORD, and thou art exalted as head above all. *(KJV)* **1 Chronicles 29:11**

And said, I beseech thee, O LORD God of heaven, the great and terrible God, that keepeth covenant and mercy for them that love him and observe his commandments: *(KJV)* **Nehemiah 1:5**

DESCRIPTION OF THE GREATNESS OF THE ALMIGHTY MOST HIGH GOD (ABBA) & THE LORD JESUS CHRIST...

GOD

is

"ALL POWERFUL"

"AWESOME"

"MAGNIFICIENT"

"AMAZING"

"PHENOMENAL"

"TREMENDOUS"

"EXCELLENT"

"QUALITY"

"BLESSED"

"PROGRESSIVE"

"RICH"

"SUPERB"

"VALUABLE"

"AUTHENTIC"

"ZENITH"

"PROSPEROUS"

"GOLDEN"

"INFINITE"

"LIGHT"

"ETHICAL"

"PINNACLE"

"EXCEPTIONAL"

"VERY ABLE"

"CREATIVE"

"WHOLESOME"

"LEGENDARY"

"ICONIC"

"WISE"

"INTELLIGENT"

"ETERNAL"

"SUPREME"

"GLORIOUS"

"HEAVENLY"

"SOVEREIGN"

BECAUSE OF HIS GREATNESS… "LET EVERYTHING THAT HAS BREATHE PRAISE YE THE LORD!!! "PSALM 150"

Praise ye the LORD. Praise God in his sanctuary:
praise him in the firmament of his power.

Praise him for his mighty acts: praise him
according to his excellent greatness.

Praise him with the sound of the trumpet:
praise him with the psaltery and harp.

Praise him with the timbrel and dance: praise him
with stringed instruments and organs.

Praise him upon the loud cymbals: praise him
upon the high sounding cymbals.

Let everything that hath breath praise the LORD. *Praise ye the* LORD.

"THE ALMIGHTY GOD IS WORTHY TO BE PRAISED!!!"

The Epilogue

I hope this *book* has been a *blessing* to you and that it has met your expectations. The purpose of writing this book was to give you the insight & understanding of the multifaceted side of the *Almighty God*. If we are not careful we will only view *God* as being just the *Creator*.

<u>*Truth of the matter*</u>-He is more than that. He is also our heavenly father who gave birth & who sustains the *Heavens & the Earth*. There are many facet and dimensions to *God* because he is *so vast, & rich in his capacity*. *The LORD* is not only the *God* of *Religion* & the *Church*. He is the *"Most High God"* Creator of all, who sits on the circle of the earth, & who has all powers in his hands. You cannot contain & put *God* in a box because he is much bigger than that. There is no definition word that can truly describe how *"Great"* and *"Awesome"* God is.

He is far beyond human comprehension because he is infinite and eternal. He operates as three persons in the *God head*. As *God* the *Father & Creator, & Jesus Christ the Son*, the *Redeemer*, & *the Holy Spirit*, the *Comforter*.

This book composition was written to give you a glimpse of the totality of *God*, as being the product. Everything that you need can be found in the *Almighty God*. He is his own entity that has the reach to fulfill every living thing on planet earth & in heaven.

The *Psalmist* was right when he said, "What is mankind that you are mindful of them & human beings that you care for them"? <u>*Psalm 8:4 (KJV)*</u>

God truly loves and appreciates his creation & he wants the best for them.

The *LORD* is in his own class but he still chooses to want to fellowship with his *Creation*. But that's the type of *God* that he is. *He commanded his love towards us while yet we were sinners.* He provided a way for humanity to interact with him through his *Son, Jesus Christ* our *Lord* & *Savior.* And because of that, now we have the access to partake in his *forgiveness, mercy and grace.*

In for that reason this book, *"He is the Product-The Almighty"* was written. So you can have a wider range perspective on *God*; as being the *Source* of everything. It's not by coincidence that you have pick up & read this *book.* I believe this book was written to *bless you, so your faith can grow stronger in the LORD.*

This is not a onetime read; this book is a guide to your lively hood that will impact your life. It will *inspire, motivate, inform, edify & encourage you.* And that's what this book offers through the information that is in it.

➢ To the *Readers*; I would like to say thank you from the bottom of my heart for reading this manuscript; *hope it is an inspiration & a blessing to you.* P̲S̲: *Author*: Dickens Saint-elien

About Author

Dickens Saint-elien is an aspiring Author, who has an *Associates degree* in *Communications* from *"Massachusetts Communication College"* in *Boston, Mass.* He also has certifications in *Office Technology* from *"A+ Computer School" in New York &* also acquires a *Business Entrepreneurship certification* from the *"Workshop in Business Opportunity"* program in *New York.*

Dickens Saint-elien is a graduate student from the *prestige school* of "Manhattan *Bible Institute*" in *New York,* where he has accomplished his religious study in *Theology.* He studied courses & received certifications at *"Manhattan Bible Institute"* in (*Evangelism), & (General Bible 1 & 2), & (Post Grad 1 & 2), & (New Testament Greek), & (Teachers Training 1 & 2), and in (Advance Pedagogy 1 & 2).*

He also received his certification in Biblical Counseling from "Kingdom Ambassadors School of Ministry" in NYC. And also received numerous (*Biblical Academic Awards*) at *"Christ Church International, & Berean Bible School of Ministry". Where he also fulfilled courses such as (Homiletics) & etc?*

Dickens Saint-elien writing ability is catered to *inspire, motivate, edify, inform & to encourage* others to be the best that they can be. He believes it is a gift that has been bestowed upon him from the *Almighty GOD & the Lord Jesus Christ.*

He is a *Minister, Teacher, Author, Inspirator & Entrepreneur* that can relate to others because he believes that we are all part of this journey called *"Life".*

For this reason he has written this prolific book *"He is the Product"-The Almighty!!!- "So he can share with you about the multifaceted side of the Almighty GOD!!!*

Bibliography

- All of the scriptures that is used in this Book was taken from the "King James Version" from the online Bible Gate Way website-(owned by Gospel Communications & Zondervan-Launched in 1993

- The Student Bible Dictionary-By Karen Dockrey and Johnnie & Phyllis Godwin-©2000 published by Barbour Publishing Uhrichsville, OH

- Google Online Dictionary & Thesaurus. Copyright 2015

- Vines Concise Dictionary of the Bible BY: Thomas Nelson Inc-Nashville, Dallas, Mexico City, Rio De Janeiro, Beijing-copyright 2005, pgs 49, 153, 243, 293

- Introducing Christian Doctrine (2nd edition) Millard J. Erickson, copyright 1992-2002-Baker Book House, published by: Baker Academic, pgs 296, 314, 321, 323, 296, 324, 333, 336, 250, 280, 295, 318, 334, 336, 359, 255, 260, 361, 362, 264, 263, 322, 312, 324, 325, 336, 334, 250, 359, 320,

Notes: